*Conversations with your home*

# Conversations with your home

## Guidance and inspiration beyond Feng Shui

## Carole J. Hyder, MA

Hyder Enterprises, Inc.
Minneapolis

Published by Hyder Enterprises, Inc.
Contact: www.carolehyder.com

Cover illustration by Carie Gross, 12 sqaured
Book design by Dorie McClelland, Spring Book Design
Author photograph by Wendy Houser Blomseth

ISBN: 978-0-9664434-4-8

Printed in the United States of America

Our house has a heart and a soul, and eyes to see us with;

and approvals and deep solicitudes and deep sympathies;

it is us and we are in its confidence, and live in its grace

and in the peace of its benediction.

We never come home from an absence

that its face does not light up and

speak out its eloquent welcome,

and we cannot enter it unmoved.

*Letters II,* Mark Twain

# Contents

*My house is me and I am it. My house is where
I like to be and it looks like all my dreams.*
—*The Big Orange Splot,* Daniel Manus Pinkwater

# Message from the Author

In most alternative modalities—like taiqi, qigong, acupuncture, feng shui—the underpinning concept is that everything is energy. Any culture that has a strong connection to nature knows this to be true. Recently, science has come around to verifying the same idea that all matter is made up of energy. When further experimentation confirmed that someone observing a phenomenon can change the actual phenomenon, the definition that "everything is energy" expanded to incorporate thoughts as well.

We are all connected through this energy which makes us part of an entire network. Our actions and our thoughts will not only affect our immediate surroundings, they will also somehow impact the black bamboo plants growing on PoTu Shan Island off the coast of China. As remote as that may seem, it may also explain why some days we move through unexplained suffering and pain. We may be feeling the impact of a grieving mother in Boston. Why would a system like this be set up anyway? Why couldn't we simply deal with our own issues, keep them for ourselves, and let everyone else do likewise? Well, we would be missing out on a very rewarding and inspiring potential.

Not only is there a connection between everything concrete and conceptual, but this connection has a consciousness of its own. Artists will share that in the midst of their creation, something happens and the artwork dictates their next move. My friend and mentor Margaret has indicated that when writing any fiction work, her characters, once developed, decide how the plot should unfold. The exhilaration of being part of a jam session with other musicians is that you get lifted out of the predictable progressions into something that no one expected. Something outside of ourselves intervenes to create a better experience, perhaps a more truthful one, but certainly a more exhilarating ride.

This interaction is not limited to artwork, novels and music, but is possible within your own home as well. There is a potential that exists in this spatial format that can open figurative doors, not just the literal ones. It is possible to establish a reciprocal rapport with your home in which you receive guidance and support, as well as discover an arena in which you can be who you truly are. Your home becomes your piece of music, the characters in your novel, your artwork—because, like all the other creative moments, it exemplifies the concept that "everything is energy."

By finding ways to connect with your home, you will be able to access the answers as well as the questions that lie within the walls. You may explore new possibilities for you and your home. You can create the life you always wanted and the life your home dreams about.

In *Conversations with Your Home,* you will have the opportunity to connect with your home. In the first section, Psychology of Space, you will have a chance to look at how your space gives you clues to who you are and, more importantly, where you are going. Your home will mirror to you a true sense of self where you can get in touch with your own core. Your home intends to help you become who you are meant to be.

In the second section, Stages of Sanctuary, you will follow your home's natural progression of life from birth to death. Over the span of twelve chapters with accompanying exercises, you will engage with your home in ways you may never have done before. There will be many points at which your connection to your home may come alive for you, whether you intend to name your home, write to your home, or accept a letter from your home.

The third section, Symbols of the Soul, underscores that your space is truly alive through the use of archetypes. This section is grounded in the premise that your home comes to you with prior energy influences. A questionnaire will help you determine which of nine archetypes your home may have captured—based on the year it was built, predecessors, remodeling projects or your own intuition.

*Conversations with Your Home* was written to let you know that you and your house are together for a higher purpose, intentional characters in the drama of life. All three sections of this book are intended to help you build and nurture a healthy and vital relationship with your home. In doing so, you will hopefully realize that you are not alone in your journey but instead are connected to a conscious energy that happens to come to you in a spatial format. This energy can help you feel whole and safe so that in the end you can create your perfect life.

# Introduction

Patty has been my esthetician for several years. A thoughtful, beautiful, and intuitive soul, she is always anxious to share stories and exchange advice. Our monthly sessions become as much therapy for one another as a treatment for my face.

One day as we were beginning our time together, Patty excitedly told me she had bought a house and was moving. Despite our indepth conversations over many, many treatments, the topic of her moving had never surfaced. In fact, I had heard comments that would lead me to believe she would never leave her beloved townhouse, for it offered her the security and sanctuary she loved and needed.

It seems one day Patty had a jarring revelation about the discouraging direction her life was taking. She decided it was time for a change. As though guided from a cosmic source, she instantly understood what she needed to do and that was move. Although it had not been a priority up to that point, moving suddenly seemed the only way to make the kind of change she wanted. While working on a less talkative client than I, she made a mental list of the features she "saw" in her new home: a particular neighborhood, space in which to move her business, beautiful back garden, specific price range. As an afterthought, she also saw a pond with a waterfall. This wasn't a wish list in Patty's mind; this was a picture of reality for her.

Her client left and Patty tried to integrate this vision that had been so clear in her mind. Her next client that day was a newly-licensed real estate agent who arrived excited and thrilled because she had her first listing. Patty off-handedly expressed interest and asked for the details while she was doing the realtor's facial. The house happened to be in the neighborhood that Patty had just "seen" and, according to the realtor, had a beautiful back garden. The realtor, still not aware that she may well be talking to a potential buyer, shared that the house was perfect for an in-home business. By now, Patty's interest is pretty intense, so she asked about the price—it was exactly in line with Patty's range. The house she had moments before seen in her mind was available. Since the realtor was her last client, Patty asked if they could see it right away.

Within 30 minutes, they were walking through the house; Patty knew this was exactly what she had seen during her vision. While they were there, Patty walked out into the beautifully landscaped back garden, amazed at how quickly her vision was coming together. The house seemed to be almost everything she had itemized in her mind. While she was taking in the charm of the land, she heard water running. The source was a small pond with a waterfall located near the door—the after-thought on her list. By the end of the day, Patty's offer was accepted.

During subsequent treatments (now in her beautiful new place), she shared with me the inspiring moments she has had with her home, and how "right" it feels to be living and working there. Always remembering the inspired vision she had before she was aware of its existence, Patty knew there was something special about the place. Before moving in, she planned to paint rooms, re-carpet, re-tile some areas, and put in a new powder room. She was very sensitive to how these enhancements would affect the home so she mentally "checked in" with the house before moving forward. All of her design decisions were a blend of her preferences overlaid with those of the house. As her furniture was moved in, she felt guided by her home to place items in a certain place. An oversized shelving unit concerned Patty because she was certain there would be no appropriate place for it. But the movers brought it in, set it in the first available spot and it fit as though it was custom-made for that corner. The whole moving-in process was a series of surprises. In the end, everything fit perfectly.

Patty shared an emotional event that occurred a few weeks after she had settled into her new home. One morning, she woke up and lay in bed admiring the beautiful paint color on the walls—a color she loved and a color she knew the house loved as well. In a half-sleep/half-awake state, she saw the walls start to move and vibrate. It was as though they were dancing around her, dancing for her, dancing with her. They seemed to wrap themselves around Patty. The love and gratitude she felt came from the very structure itself. It was at that moment that she knew the house had sought her out specifically and together, at that unsuspecting moment, they celebrated the event. "The bedroom came alive!" she said smiling through tears as she told me the story. "My house is alive!"

Although I had experienced a similar connection to my own home, I attributed it to my extensive experience with Feng Shui. I had implemented a lot of intentional changes within its walls for which I regularly felt reciprocal responses. It didn't occur to me that anyone else might tap into their own space to such a similar degree—until Patty relayed her own story. I realized that it wasn't my private privilege to have a dynamic relationship with my home. The reason I write this book is to teach you how to find your own way to bring your house to life so you can savor the moment when you wake up some morning to the dynamic dance you and your home have created together and can likewise say "My house is alive!"

Feng Shui (fung shway) is the study of space in the context of the people who live or work there. This perspective originates from China and, in conservative terms, has at least a 2500-year legacy. There is known documentation that emperors used Feng Shui to set up their palaces for maximum success, luck, and longevity. The principles of yin-yang and the 5 Elements were all incorporated into the Feng Shui considerations of a place, along with directionality factors that included the struc-ture itself and the birth data of the individuals. An overlay of all this information determined whether someone would have a happy life in a particular spot or not.

I was first introduced to the concept of Feng Shui in 1992 and was almost instantly propelled into being an "expert" because of local demand. At the time I was also owner of a design business that was busy, demanding and pretty reward-ing at times. I had no expectations of making Feng Shui a career. However, three years later, I had an opportunity to sell the business, enabling me to see if Feng Shui was worthy of pursuit other than on a personal basis.

By 1998 I had written my first book and was putting

together a formal certification program for training others in the art of Feng Shui. During this time, I facilitated hundreds of Feng Shui appointments—residential and commercial, small offices, corporations, restaurants, married people, single people, divorcing people. As part of my training, and the training I in turn impart to my own students, I learned to pay attention to space and what it says in relation to our own lives. I learned, and now teach, how to manipulate features, both design and architectural, to enhance people's lives.

While I was studying Feng Shui, I naturally made some adjustments in my own home. The more adjustments I made the more "real" my house felt. It seemed like we were forming a relationship, my home and me. One day I decided to give it a name. I felt good about doing that and it seemed to solidify for me a tangible bond.

I made a regular and conscious effort to tune in from time to time. Having no expectations of what would result from this action, I simply remained open. Occasionally I would feel something. It seemed to happen when I was doing some inconsequential activity, like walking down the stairs, or coming in the front door, or moving around the kitchen. It would make me pause for a moment and look for a reason for these feelings. I wondered if the house had become haunted.

A Gallup poll taken in June 2009 determined that 37% of Americans believe in ghosts, 1% point higher than those who believe in global warming. I knew from my experience doing Feng Shui consultations that when an entity took up residence in a home it wasn't usually positive. Doors were opening and closing at will, items were moved around, and lights were going on and off. Any logical explanations for these activities were eliminated. Although some of my clients described their ghosts as benign, the feeling I was getting in my house was more than "benign," it was soft and respectful. Nothing bizarre was happening around the house, just a sense of something familiar and comfortable. To test my theory that these feelings may be coming from my house, I decided to reach out.

I started by asking for advice regarding decisions specific to the house: What should I do with this closet? What about this bothersome squeak in the floor? What if we take out these cabinets? I would then wait for some response. Sometimes I had an immediate "aha" moment and knew what to do. Once I woke up from a dream with the answer to one of my questions. Other times I had to wait for guidance to appear in the form of a hunch. No matter how I got the information, it was always appropriate and effective—and didn't come from anything on my radar screen. It was as though an idea or suggestion was dropped in "out of the blue."

Then I asked about items within the house. Is this a good place for the dresser? Does this window need a curtain? Is this the best color for the hall? Again, I always arrived at good answers. I have serious doubts I would have arrived at the hall-way color on my own. The color was not my first choice, but turned out beautifully and perfectly. Something or someone seemed to inform that decision other than me.

Finally, I focused my questions entirely on things of a more personal nature, nothing specific about the house itself. How should I answer this student's desperate question? What is the meaning of this difficult situation? Where will I be able to find the help that I need? While I may have asked the questions in a state of panic or anxiety, the answers were always thoughtful and direct, consistent and honorable. They came from a place of compassion and patience, definitely not the place from which I was often asking. It was at this point that I made a commitment to the belief that my house was alive and wanted to be acknowledged. I promised myself (and the house) I would remain open and listen as best I could.

While at first I was the one asking questions about anything and everything, from life-altering possibilities (Should I write this book?) to mundane things (Should we repair the garage door?) I was surprised the first time the house prompted me with a question. I didn't know where exactly the question came from nor did I know how to respond to it. Hanging up from a phone conversation with a client, I heard a tersely worded "Why aren't you writing?" Since no one was in the room at the time except one of my cats, I had only one explanation of the origin of this question. The house was making a point about my lack of time devoted to writing this book and wondering why I found ways to avoid such important work. We began a hesitant dialogue in that moment—the hesitation was entirely on my side; I thought perhaps I was exhausted and imagining the communication. However, the next day, another conversation came about ("Fix the window please")—referring to a window that needed repair.

For quite a while my house and I found lots of reasons to check in with one another every day. Our conversations varied in length depending on the situation. Sometimes we only needed a few moments to connect with one another, sometimes a lot more time was devoted to a specific topic. This phase of daily interchanges went on for several months, as though we were catching up on long years of silence.

Today our dialogue has moved into a softer pace, which includes times of silence knowing we will no longer lose touch. It may be days before either of us feels the need to make contact. Sometimes I hear a question coming from the walls wondering why I haven't taken action in a certain direction. Sometimes I express concern about the condition of some part of the house, making a promise to get it repaired. At night, however, I'm very aware of its quiet presence holding me while I sleep.

I am discovering how to work with this new kind of relationship—a mirror of who I am. It's a connection which will change as I change, yet brings with it a universal wisdom otherwise unreachable. It's a relationship that isn't co-dependent—the house doesn't make me feel guilty when I go away for a few days. I don't pine uncontrollably when I have to leave. But it welcomes me back unconditionally each time I arrive home, whether coming from the grocery store or a two-week trip to Asia. I listen for comments and guidance. Mostly I feel its creative potential expressing itself in quiet, subtle ways. Not wanting to control my life nor tell me how to do everything to perfection, it reaches out just as a dear friend would. My home wants to stay healthy and whole and, in doing so, will help me in return.

Once the connection between me and my home developed and solidified, other homes took the opportunity to express themselves to me. These dialogues were often short and focused, but a message was being sent, which I would then pass along to my client. I was inexplicably overcome in a home of one client who had me come over because something "just wasn't right" about her house. Sitting in her house, I was overwhelmed with feelings of loneliness. When I mentioned this to her, she assured me she wasn't suffering from loneliness; on the contrary she loved the solitude of living alone. Before she bought the house, it had sat empty for several years. In fact, it had been neglected by renters, had several broken or cracked windows, and a roof that leaked. There was a definite loneliness in the air that evidently did not belong to the client. We could only conclude that her house was lonely. Based on the premise that a house and its occupant will eventually blend their energy, it wouldn't have been long before she would have integrated these negative sentiments into her own life. Knowing this, she came up with a meaningful ritual to start her own conversation with her home in order to help her house heal.

Another client was struggling with a life-threatening illness. Clarisse was undertaking countless ways to cure herself, traveling, despite her weakened condition, to faraway places because she heard of a procedure that might work. She was about to go to Europe because of yet another possibility, a trip she could hardly afford money-wise or energy-wise. It was at this point she asked me to help her with the Feng Shui in her home. When I was there, I heard a near-palpable sob which seemed to come from someplace within the house. I didn't mention it but asked if we could walk through the space. We moved through her rooms until I found the one which I knew produced the sound. I asked Clarisse about this room—it was, in fact, her favorite room although it was not her bedroom. As I stood in there, I knew her home wanted this to be a healing room. Her home could and would heal her if only she'd listen. My client had built this home years ago—understandably, a long-term relationship between them had been built as well. The "sob" expressed the sadness of what may happen if she continued to turn away from the healing that was possible right under her nose, right down the hall.

I shared with Clarisse what I felt her home was saying to me—that it wanted to help her heal and specifically in this room. She spent a few moments in silence looking at me and looking around at the room. "Of course," she said, "this makes perfect sense." She cancelled any further travel plans and set up the room to help her heal, which it eventually did.

The longer I did my Feng Shui work, I discovered that in implementing Feng Shui principles, I had ignored one element that was crucial to improving someone's life—and that was the feedback from the home. Feng Shui was being done to the home, not with the home—a big difference in terms of outcome. Homes are energetically vital, they want to help, they love to protect, they will support and encourage—if only we could hear their whispers. A home will often entice a person to move in to provide them the experience relevant and crucial to their individual journey. Likewise, a home will let the owner know when it's time to move on. I've seen desperate homes take desperate actions to get attention, hoping someone will hear them and acknowledge them. I've felt the frustration of a house as it tried to nudge people toward a beneficial direction but who, in the end, just couldn't hear the message. An unfulfilled house is one that is not allowed to be part of their owners' lives.

Their messages are delicate and sensitive, usually lost in the noise of our lives. Unfortunately we are just not tuned in to their vernacular. However, your home can be your best friend. In fact that's all it wants—to be recognized as a friend. It can be the support you need, the connection to your inner truth, the light in the window. It can be an untapped source of insight for your day-to-day issues or life-altering ones. In turn, the home only asks for recognition, for care, and for some of our time.

A home's ultimate purpose, besides being a shelter, is to prompt our memory as to who we are and what our fundamental truth entails. A home is the place that lets you be you, that knows you well, that knows you at your core. A home holds the template of our thoughts. As our thoughts change, so does our home; as home changes, so do our thoughts.

It is possible for everyone to awaken to the identity and consciousness that is alive within their space. This will be a mutual relationship, each taking care of one another. The more you care for your home, the more you will benefit from its perceptions. By making this crucial connection, you can not only access the answers to your own questions, but also provide answers to the questions the house may be asking. Together you and your home can work toward being the best that you both can be.

Without fail, whenever I mentioned to someone that I was writing a book about having conversations with a home, this announcement provoked two sequential responses. The first reaction was surprise at the idea of conversing with a space— they would express concern that I wouldn't find enough material to fill an actual book. However, this was typically followed by a story—from childhood, from recent history, from current time—about a special home, a place that they loved, a place that seemed to speak to them in a unique and profound way. It was always an experience they never forgot and in some way changed them. By the end of their own story about their home, these same doubtful individuals would understand my reasons for this book. Some of their  stories were used to fill these very pages.

So, I ask that you keep an open mind as we explore the idea that your home may be alive. What if your house was more than sheet-rock and siding? What if it was more than carpeting and closets? What if behind those walls was a sweet spirit waiting for you to listen? Over the years, what we would call "inanimate" objects have become more and more alive in our eyes. Pets have become like children to some people, with a form of communication happening on both sides—they're no longer just farm animals. There's scientific data that plants relate to the sounds in their environment. People name their cars giving them qualities that would normally be used for people. As part of a normal awakening progression, I suggest you try listening to your home. With a small amount of effort, you, too, like Patty, will be able to say, "yes, my house is alive!

# Preliminary Preparation

## A Scrapbook of Your Home

A beginning action that can help solidify and support the exercises in this section is to start a scrapbook of your home. It can be an on-going project that covers a span of time—from when you moved in to the present. Appropriate items to include are a blueprint (or a hand-drawn floor plan), the deed, photos of the house, pictures of family events in the house. Along with that, you will now have a place to chronicle and store information that comes up relevant to the exercises and the archetypes.

Just as we make scrapbooks for each of our children, here is an opportunity to make one for your home. Have fun with this project and keep it light-hearted. With an entire industry built around making scrapbooks, a lot of possibilities are available for making this not only an attractive presentation but also an outstanding collection of facts and memories based on your home.

Purchase a scrapbook you feel best expresses the connection to your home. It might be a certain color—one that matches the color of your house—or size. You may opt to have one where you can insert a photo of your home on the front cover.

This is not the time to buy a cheap version or in any way cut corners. It's possible you might leave the scrapbook on your coffee table or somewhere obvious where visitors and family can look at it. Even if you feel it's too personal for just anyone's eyes, you will still want to honor what you're creating with an attractive and respectful presentation. Recording the images and memories of your home deserves a first-class appearance.

Once you have the right scrapbook, you gather everything related to your home that you might want to put within its pages. Some of these items will result from the exercises in this book but other items might be specific to your home and you simply need a place to keep them.

Include photographs of your house from when you first moved in or as far back as you can obtain. Placing photos according to a time-frame is a logical way to visually see the story of the house and to note its changes. But there may be other ways you'll want to view your home. You may decide you want to access information according to particular rooms. You may want a special section just for the outside. You may want to focus on the front entry through a whole series of changes. There is no prescribed way this has to happen.

If you don't already have a blueprint or deed of your home, sometimes those can be obtained from a city or county office. There are services that will trace the history of your house, complete with a copy of the deed and original floor plan. Doing an internet search will provide you with many options. You can also draw your own version of your home, whether exactly to scale or not.

Many of the exercises you will read about suggest you write down words or phrases. You will also be encouraged to write letters to your home and you may also receive some information from your home which you'll want to keep for future reference.

Don't forget to include receipts for work done that was particularly special to you; or small pieces of wallpaper used in the dining room; or paint samples; or catalog pictures of the special light fixtures in the dining room. Anything relevant to you and scrapbook-appropriate (as in, "flat") should be considered for inclusion.

The album could not only record the past and the current home, but it can also address the future. This would entail writing your thoughts about what you want to do someday—when you have more time, when you have more money, when the kids move out, etc. You may even cut out photographs of how a particular room would look in the future, or how you'd like the landscape to develop. A future remodel project can be recorded prior to it becoming reality.

By chronicling the history of your home, you may be surprised at the changes that have occurred over the years, or how little it has changed. If you haven't lived in your home very long, you can record the changes you still want to make happen. A scrapbook can become a great place to store some of the data about your home, where it will be organized and accessible. It can also become a log or journal of memories about what it was like to have a conversation with your house.

# *Psychology of Space*
## Home is a Reflection of Your Life

Architecture is to make us know
and remember who we are.
—Sir Jellicoe Geoffrey (1900–1996),
English landscape architect

Carl Jung (1875–1961, Swiss psychiatrist and founder of analytical psychology) gave us a crucial and pivotal gift through time that simply states "the unconscious seeks outward manifestation." In his autobiography *Memories, Dreams, and Reflections,* Jung recounts the story of building his home on Lake Zurich as an expression of his unconscious into solid form. In 1923, he constructed a simple round tower which he called home. Over a period of approximately 30 years, he built four additions onto the original tower—another tower, a courtyard, a second floor, and some additional structures. In his words, his home became a place where "I am in the midst of my true life, I am most deeply myself." Each phase marked a new evolution in his own life, reflecting a way to express his internal condition.

Your home likewise gives you clues as to where you are and where you are going. You may create your environment, but it is in the reflection of that environment that you see what you may not ordinarily discover about yourself. Your environment mirrors to you what is called a sense of self, where you get in harmony with your own core. Your home helps you become who you are meant to be.

I have three goals in writing this book: one is to give the message that your home is alive and holds a consciousness. Although it may physically look like a static structure, it is far from inert; it is alive and vital. It welcomes and appreciates any attention and intention you throw its way. Even people who would argue with this idea can't deny the experience of walking into a space that has been "awakened." They usually can't pinpoint what exactly makes the space feel special, they just know it does.

The second goal for *Conversations with Your House* is to offer the idea that the house doesn't just take the positive favors that you give them, but it can also reciprocate and return your favors in unexpected, heartfelt, even charming ways. There is positive reinforcement for all that you may do to make the space better. Like any balanced relationship, there is give and take on both sides. It isn't just about you taking care of it; often it's all about it taking care of you. We just don't realize that's what is happening.

Besides its obvious job of keeping you safe and warm, a house takes care of you by reminding you of who you are and what you love. The best compliment a home can receive is to witness a visitor looking around and saying: "This house is so YOU!" Mission accomplished. The two of you have worked together to create something that can uphold your values, your dreams, and can even reflect where you're going. For those who can see, the space has become a road map showing where you are now and where you intend to head in the future.

Margaret Lulic, author of *Home–Inspired by Love and Beauty* describes this process well. She says, "A loving home is the unity of a specific dwelling, all those people and things that it shelters, and the sense of treasuring and being treasured. In its fullest form, everything about the home has been conceived in love and inspired by beauty—not just the physical aspects—but the relationships, values, and daily rituals. The result is the happiness that Aristotle argues is the deepest desire of humanity. This is not just the happiness of pleasure or peace of mind; it is the happiness of participation in something meaningful. The act of conceiving arises from your inner life of imagination, understanding, and creativity."

When I decided to go back to graduate school to get a
Masters in East Asian Studies, I knew I would need to carve
out a place to study. I couldn't expect my current office to hold
an enormous project like that. Before my classes started in the
fall, I walked around our home asking "Where would a graduate student study?" I had to ignore my logical side that told
me there was no other room for me to study except my office.
I projected ahead to being the student and looked for a place
that would reflect that new part of me. My house lost no time
in guiding me to the living room/guest room on the lower
level which was used very intermittently and could easily and
effectively be turned into my study area. I hadn't considered it
as appropriate since I used it for meetings (very occasionally)
and we had overnight guests (once or twice a year). These were
both activities we could maneuver around when needed.

I spent many an hour in that room over three years of
course work and found it to be the perfect place. It had its
own fireplace, adequate room for a desk, storage area, and
a sofa for times when I wanted to stretch out and read with
one of my cats. The fond memories of those years spent in
that room still come up when I go in there. It was a happy day
when I graduated, but I must admit a bittersweet moment
when I returned the room to its original state. My home had
adjusted to satisfying my own goals in a way that surpassed
what I had hoped to find. It took on my dream and reflected
it to me daily. When the dream was accomplished, we both
moved on to other things.

Everything in your space will either reflect where you are,
where you want to go, or where you were. The latter aspect is
the one to monitor carefully because, without you realizing

it, your space can hold you back. I'm reminded of the adage about the carpenter who blames his shoddy workmanship on his tools. If you set up out-dated tools and reminders around your home, then it's possible you will not end up where you want. Your life will take on the imprint of past ideas, past relationships, past beliefs. If you let your home remain behind, reflecting a phase of your life you'd like to forget, you'll be mired in the past no matter how much you want to move forward. Keep your home "current" with an eye toward the future and you will follow suit.

The third goal for writing *Conversations with Your House* is to seed the idea that your house had a life and history of its own, before you came along. It brings with it the influence of the time during which it was built, the conditions under which it was constructed, and the way it was used prior to your occupancy. Your house has its own story which must factor into yours. It doesn't come to you as a perfectly clean slate. This doesn't mean some of the difficulties it endured or witnessed can't be mitigated, but even the positive aspects can influence the way you live in the space. By adding your dreams with the experiences of your home, you have the makings of a rich and rewarding relationship.

Consciousness in a structure is different than consciousness as we know and observe in humans. Humans are endowed with awareness, free will, and the ability to make decisions. Nevertheless, this should not be a reason to minimize the kind of life or spirit your home holds. Without the responsibility of decision-making, your space holds a continual connection to universal order. There is a direct knowingness and clarity that your space can provide since it's unencumbered with having to weigh options. Of course, as humans, it's important that we have this gift of choice for it provides us lessons and brings us satisfaction. But it also can muddy the water. We strive our whole lives to attain the simplicity of this divine connection so that clarity and wisdom can be ours. We only need to look at our walls to see the possibilities.

Homes are taken for granted, yet we all know there is some unspoken importance. In the 1950s movie *It's a Wonderful Life,* the house was one of the main characters in the story. In the beginning, we see its decrepit, run-down condition as an abandoned home. The two main characters, George and Mary, even throw rocks at its windows. Yet the house clearly has some magical powers since they somehow know the house will grant them their wish if their rock successfully blows out one of the windows. The scene of the wedding night dinner indicates the extent of its deterioration.

Over time, the movie narrates how the house changes right along with their lives and is eventually filled with children. When the community rallies around George's misfortune, the culminating scene takes place in this house. The top of the banister becomes a touchpoint for the story. For some reason, it never got permanently fixed in place and is a constant source of annoyance to George, that is, until he has an epiphany and realizes he may have lost his house and his life forever. Suddenly that loose banister top is precious and endearing to him. Nothing drives home his change of heart more than the moment when he grabs the loose top and kisses it. George has fallen back in love with his life and his home.

*The notion of buildings that speak helps us to place*
*at the very center of our architectural conundrums*
*the question of the values we want to live by—*
*rather than merely of how we want things to look.*
—*The Architecture of Happiness*, Alan deBotton

## Your Forward-Thinking Home

You give your home permission to guide you forward or hold you back, whether you know it or not. To help you discover what your home may be saying about you, here is an exercise to see if your dream and your home are synchronized. Once it's completed, you will get insight into the current messages your home is whispering (or shouting) to you and how you can get those messages more in line with your new image.

### Is my house leading me to my future?

Get a pen and paper and plan to spend 30–40 minutes of uninterrupted time. Spend a few moments, clearing your mind of distractions and tuning into the spirit of your home. This will be an opportunity to ask yourself a question and let your house answer it for you. The question is based on where you see yourself next, what you want to be doing in the future, and how you want your ideal life to play out. This could address a future career or advancement in your current one, or it might address some qualities you want to strive toward.

Create a statement about how you'd like your life to evolve by answering the question "What would my ideal life look like?" Answers might be something like:

I am a published author.
I am the owner of a successful business.
I am blissfully retired in Mexico.
I am the consummate traveler.
I enjoy creating and successfully selling my artwork.
I see that everyone treats me with respect.

Once you've got your statement securely in mind, write it down. Then, rephrase your statement into a question, such as:

Does this home reflect a successful author?
Is this the home of a successful business owner?
Does this home reflect someone who is blissfully retired?
Is this the home of a consummate traveler?

Walk through your home, room-by-room, observing your furniture, wall color, rugs or carpet, lighting, the presence of clutter, artwork, etc. As you do, keep posing your question.

Let your home reflect to you what your message is all about. If the answer to your question is "yes" (as in, "Yes, it does reflect the home of a successful author," etc.) then you are probably feeling good about your space. It is supporting your current dream. But ask yourself if there is something more you may want to do or be. Is there another step you could take to keep yourself and your space moving forward?

Make a note of the things that are in contradiction to your dream statement. Don't worry about whether you can do anything about them just yet, simply write them down. If you don't like your sofa, then write "sofa" on your paper; if you hate the wall color in your bedroom, write "bedroom paint."

Once you've been through your home, sit down and

prioritize those aspects that contradict or do not support your dream, from the most offensive to the least offensive. You might think the paint on your bedroom walls is childish yet kind of fun, but you're really upset by the condition of the dining room table. The dining room table would be higher on the list than the bedroom wall color.

Go through your list one-by-one and decide if there's some action you can take to change that specific condition in your home that is not in agreement with your dream statement. If the sofa is falling apart and doesn't reflect your dream of wanting more respect, you can decide if you want to replace it, put a slip cover on it, get new pillows, or have no sofa at all. Don't settle for something just because you should or because it's a change. You want to ascertain that the change is ultimately helping you move forward into the life that you want.

Fashion provides a parallel example. Typically, we try to keep our wardrobe up-to-date and stylish, but because the dress bought last year will be out-dated by next year, it is an ongoing process. We accept it as a fact of life, becoming accustomed to looking for new things to wear so that we don't seem out-dated. If we want to be fashionable and stylish, we have to be vigilant about trends, factoring in what we like and what is flattering. This same philosophy should be carried over to your home. It is also a process which means if you've got the same color on the walls that you've had for 20 years, it may be time for a change. If you've got the same bedraggled lamp sitting on the night stand that you had as a child, it may be time to consider something more up-to-speed as to who you are now and who you want to be.

It isn't always necessary to spend a fortune to update. Just as in fashion a belt or scarf can change the entire look; in your home a few new pillows or a new lampshade can make a difference. Through all these changes, keep in mind your question: Does this item/color/home match my dream?

I'm reminded of a friend whose dream was to get into a healthy, satisfying relationship. Bonnie dated a lot of men over the years, but couldn't seem to find the right match. She had a beautiful rolltop desk in an area in her home that corresponds to Relationships. I knew that one of the past boyfriends had given it to her—he had used it for many years but decided he was going to purchase something new. Bonnie happily took it. However, each time she sat at that desk, she was reminded of this difficult past relationship. So, at my suggestion, she got rid of it, although she sorely needed a desk for her work.

A month or so later, she let me know she had acquired another desk that she was thrilled about. It was modern, relatively new, fit in the corner better than the other one, etc., etc. When I asked about its origin, she told me it came from her ex-husband. Unfortunately, Bonnie had not improved her situation at all, having exchanged one desk from a doomed relationship with another one having the same history.

You can walk through your whole home asking your question; however, there are some key areas in which this exercise will be most effective. The main one is your bedroom because that is often the room that gets left behind and also because it's the room where you dream. Another area where this exercise will have some impact is in the entry to your home. This is the room of first impressions and could be crucial in setting a new tone. If you're working on career shifts, your office will be instrumental in supporting your dream.

# Home as Healer

The following narrative is reminiscent of the *Tao Te Ching* statement that says "Without leaving your home, you can know the whole world" (Lao Tzu, chapter 47). This is a story about a woman who found herself by not leaving home. In fact, she spent three years inside the same four walls, absorbing what the space provided her.

Several years ago I worked with a woman named Astrid who shared with me that she recently spent three years inside her condominium. She truly never left. She ordered the things she needed online—groceries, clothes, furniture. Through the use of the computer she could work from home. She opened the door to delivery people and that was it. Somehow she hadn't completely lost contact with her family, or even a few friends, who kept in touch via phone and email. Eventually, their urging for her to get some help prompted Astrid to take action so she could live a more normal life. Besides professional counseling, having a Feng Shui appointment was part of that turnaround.

Astrid shared that she hadn't been afraid to go out—not at all. In times past, she enjoyed shopping for clothes, going to grocery stores, and searching out bargains at flea markets. Now that she had been able to turn that behavior around, she enjoyed those activities again. No, Astrid hadn't been afraid of going out, she had been afraid of leaving. She had created a space that suited her, that had all her favorite things and her favorite colors. It was a familiar place—something she could count on. She was afraid if she left, it wouldn't be there when she got back. By staying home, she was assured of security.

Understandably, childhood circumstances left Astrid

scarred. Countless times she remembered when she had to pack up her toys and her clothes in the middle of the night to avoid an angry landlord or bill collectors. She would just get settled into a place, make friends, find her way to school, when she'd have to start all over. As an adult, once she found a place she loved, she unconsciously decided she would never take that chance again. Because her job enabled her to work from home, several weeks passed before she realized she had not been out of her condo—and she liked it that way. Before long, Astrid was making excuses to family and friends for why she couldn't meet them or have them over.

Astrid assured me she never stopped keeping her condo in order through the years of isolation. She kept it clean, typically cooked for herself, and ordered in whatever else she may need. She never felt as though she was in prison— she just did not want to leave. As I sat in her kitchen while she fixed us both some tea, I asked her to check in with her condo to see if there were any messages for her about the experience. Admittedly, she was surprised at the idea but spent a few moments "tuning in."

At first she didn't seem to understand the exercise and would open her eyes and say things like: "What's supposed to happen here?" "I'm not getting anything." "I don't think my house wants to talk." But when I gave her permission to let go of the exercise and open her eyes, she had plenty to say. In fact, her eyes filled with tears as she told me how grateful she was to her condo for seeing her through a difficult and unusual time.

She shared that for the first time, she was in a place she loved and one that loved her. She felt comfortable and safe in putting down roots in order to heal some dark wounds. She figured that any other place would not have put up with her decision to stay inside for such an extended period of time. This was her own journey and, lucky for her, she had a safe place to let it unfold. Not once did she feel her condo was keeping her from leaving—it embraced her no matter what she chose to do.

If my client Astrid had lived somewhere else, would the outcome have been the same? Would she have found the same support somewhere else? Unlikely. On some level, she felt the safety net her condo could provide in order for her to play out and heal a difficult time she experienced as a child. In a different place, the process would probably have been different; we are different people in different places. Another space may not have been as patient. But here with this condo, there was an unspoken understanding that Astrid felt, giving her the go-ahead to move into uncharted territory. If Astrid had moved into a place that needed repairs or needed healing of its own, perhaps from some difficult predecessors or from being left unoccupied, I dare say she would not have gotten the subconscious endorsement she needed.

Astrid intends to stay in her condo indefinitely. She comes and goes freely now, confident in the knowledge that her place will be there when she returns. She has named her place and writes letters to it frequently, her heart filled with gratitude for the part it played in her healing.

People generally select their homes from a subconscious level. They may be drawn to a place and can't always verbalize why. Even when they can specifically outline what they like about a particular piece of property, I've discovered that there are always other factors which are typically unknown to the buyer. As in Astrid's case—did she think she might check out for a few years so went looking for the place that would make it possible? I think not. Did the space entice her to invest her money and then provide her some options, one of which was to stay home? I think that's possible.

Our spaces are a reminder of what we're here to work on. It is usually an emotional decision to invest in a particular piece of property, just as it is choosing a mate. This courting dance between a potential buyer and a home is a personal one because each space brings with it a potential for a lesson or for a situation to unfold. The majority of buyers are oblivious to this underlying circumstance, moving forward based on their gut feelings. And just as well, because often what lies ahead may look like too much of a challenge for most people.

Somehow the subconscious guides someone into a space that will continue to challenge their health, or their money, or their ability to sustain a relationship, or whatever they've been working on. Moving from one place to another will not leave someone's issues behind. In fact, a move to a new home can exacerbate the issue—and that is the point. A home that is good at helping people heal a relationship issue may indeed bring that issue to the forefront in such a way that the owner can't do anything but look at it. The house isn't asking someone to leave or trying to get them out just because there's an increase in their pain; it is asking them to heal. The psychological relationship between a person and their space is meant to bring out the best in both of them.

When someone moves into a space where there are challenges in a specific area, I know there's a lesson at hand. It doesn't mean they always have to plunge into the desperate depths of the issue but it does mean the space is giving them a gift—a chance to look at the matter, work out the unresolved, and rise above its physical manifestation. The house is there to help someone do just that.

Ben bought a small attractive home while he was going through a divorce. A big challenge he was facing was his ex-wife's demand for money. He was already paying child support, giving her their home and furnishings, turning over most of the retirement savings, and yet she wanted more. Based on Feng Shui principles, there were three major challenges in the money area of Ben's new home: a fireplace, a missing piece, and a back door. These features symbolically matched his current situation: money was being burned up (by the position of the fireplace); money was "missing" (mirrored by the missing area of the house); and the money that he did earn had a direct path out of his life (through the back door). *See Addendum B, What is Feng Shui? on page 203 for more information about the principles of Feng Shui.*

As we discussed the reality of his home, Ben was discouraged and angry that he had walked into a scenario that echoed the situation around his failing marriage—money challenges. He was furious with himself at how much he had given to his ex-wife and wondered why he hadn't taken a stand for his own needs and demands. It was her idea to get a divorce, after all. Ben was exasperated by the fact that he runs out of money before his next paycheck, despite the fact that he is one of the highest paid employees at his company. Certainly the help of a therapist provided insights to his beliefs. And a Feng Shui consultation added more information and ideas.

It is my experience that living in a space which requires you to pay attention to a compromised area is the best way to learn about that issue. As you make Feng Shui adjustments in the afflicted area, you see them as symbols for what needs to be changed. As he hung a mirror over his fireplace, Ben saw this as a symbol for him to say "no" to his ex-wife. As he planted a lush and healthy plant in the missing money area outside the house, he saw that as a metaphor for committing to his budget no matter what. Hanging a windchime by his backdoor in the money area was a continual alarm clock to remind him about rebuilding his own nest egg.

For the first time, he watched his patterns and his emotions and was able to forecast when he might let down his financial boundaries, falling into a vulnerable spending spree. He came to appreciate his money and treated it with respect. Ben realized that his house, bought in a split second of despair, had provided him "opportunities" to turn his issue around. It was the steady presence of this little home, without judgment or impatience, which enabled him to dig deep and find some answers—and change a lifelong pattern. As Ben saw it, the challenged money area in his house became an asset to him.

Having a space hold your intention is its best contribution. It won't withhold its support or take back promises made to you when you moved in. Ben, like most of us, probably would have shied away from a home where long-held beliefs were going to unravel—had he known. Luckily, we usually don't know what lies ahead as we excitedly set up our lives into a new space we're going to call home.

When a perspective buyer has a lot of positive and upbeat energy around a space or when a sale goes through effortlessly and snag-free, then owner and home have found each other.

Interfering in someone's decision to buy a specific piece of property may likely change a path that is crucial for them to take. It is only our interpretation that when things start to go wrong or when someone's life suddenly seems to be in disarray that the house is somehow jinxed and the move was a mistake. This is the time to figure out how to work with the potential that is being offered, not how to get out of there.

No matter what structural or design "issue" a space may have, it provides the owner with an opportunity. The chance to discover their own resistance or blind spot around a certain area in their lives and to work it through within the familiarity of a space who knows them well is a blessing. I encourage my clients to embrace the issues their house presents, come to understand them, see where the weaknesses are in their own lives, and what it is they have to discover about the matter to bring about a positive resolution.

> We live in our homes and they live in us.
> —Carole Hyder

## A Home's Influence on Your Childhood

If you think back to your childhood home, many patterns and imprints were put in place during that time that you no doubt carry over to your current home. If you were one of the lucky ones and have happy memories of your childhood home, no doubt some of those same features or patterns make you feel comfortable now. Or it may explain why you may be uncomfortable in your current home since it may be lacking the kind of familiar embrace that you long for. It's also possible you feel comfortable in a home that is similar to the one in which you grew up even if your childhood was pretty miserable. The familiarity outweighs the painful triggers. It is not uncommon to dream that you're living in your childhood home as an adult. Its impact is more profound than anyone may think. Clare Cooper Marcus in her book *House as a Mirror of Self* states that it's "in the environments of childhood that the person we are today began to take shape."

My sister and I had the opportunity to visit a house we had both lived in growing up. I lived there from age 1 to 9, so obviously many of my childhood memories came from that time frame and that house. During some of my visits back to my hometown I had driven by the house but never knew who lived there. I saw how they had changed the front porch and had built a two-car garage. They painted it yellow and added shutters. It seemed like they were taking good care of it and that was all that mattered.

One day my sister accidentally realized that the woman she was talking to at a social event lived in our old house. The woman graciously welcomed us to visit the house whenever we wanted, so on one of my trips back to my old stomping grounds we called her. I figured we'd walk through, recognize some features, not recognize others, see what changes they had made and leave. I hadn't expected we'd be there for over an hour while I was flooded with memories from the house.

From the minute we walked in, I remembered things I hadn't thought about for years or since we'd moved out. I remembered immediately where my parents put the piano and their first TV set. I remembered my little red chair that was always on the porch where I would play (where IS that chair?). I remembered our rose-colored couch and matching chairs that we gave away when we moved into our new house.

When we walked into what was once my bedroom, I turned to my sister and reminded her of the times she'd make up bedtime stories for me. I remembered the metal lamp that was clamped on the headboard. In the basement, I remembered my mother washing clothes. In the backyard I remembered a circular petunia bed my dad had planted, outlined in white painted stones. When I got upstairs I remembered the slumber parties my sister had when I was little while I was downstairs trying to sleep.

I remembered having the measles in my bedroom and the balloons my dad brought me. The back door was in a different place but I was able to point out to the current owners where it was when I lived there and even found a small indication that it had indeed existed in that spot. Even features that they had changed didn't stop me from telling them how it used to be— there was a cupboard right HERE that held Oreo cookies.

When we got out in the car my sister looked at me with some concern that I had gotten a little carried away. The experience was different for her since there are nearly 14 years between us—her experience in that house was different and short-lived. The house had indeed come alive for me, nudging my memories into life as well. It wasn't that the memories were painful, it was just that there were so many of them. Where had they been all this time? Stored in the walls, waiting for someone to recognize and validate their existence. On my own, I wouldn't have been able to do that. But with the help of some subtle murmurs, I was able to recall a cascade of childhood patterns. I have no doubt the house enjoyed the afternoon as much as I did.

One of the childhood memories many people have is creating a secret place where they could go to be alone or to invite special people. After living in the house described above, we moved to a new home that my parents built. I wasn't allowed much freedom in my space growing up—the walls of my room were painted a certain color, the bedspread matched along with corresponding pillows. I didn't realize I didn't like the color until much later when I was able to make my own paint selections. My room was my mother's taste and selections and I got to sleep in it.

One day I went up to our unheated attic to retrieve something my mother needed and saw there a small dressing table that was being stored. I don't know where it came from—it seemed like it could have been something my dad made at one time. It had curtains on the front rather than doors and there was a little chair that went with it. I had to have it. My mother pointed out that it didn't go with the colors in my room and there was no good place to put it and, furthermore, what did I want with that old thing?

It remained in the attic but I went to visit it regularly. Those were magical moments when I would bundle up and go up to sit in the little chair. Sometimes I was an actress, putting on my makeup for the next scene, memorizing my lines, giving autographs. Sometimes I was the executive secretary, writing important letters, filing top-secret documents, answering the phone, falling in love with my boss. Other times I went up to write in my diary or to write a letter to my pen pal.

My dressing table was more than a place to play out

imaginative scenarios. I became untouchable up there. My mother would stand at the bottom of the stairs trying to lure me down with cookies or with common sense about how cold it was. I was immovable. I had created a world which fed me more than cookies ever could—a world where I belonged. The sky was the limit when I was there—there was nothing I couldn't do or be. In my mind I often go back to those afternoons in the attic and try to recapture the exhilaration I felt there.

This childhood place may be the first time we get in touch with who we are, before family expectations come into play, before we're influenced by our friends' decisions, and before we succumb to societal parameters. Most people remember some kind of special private place—often a secret one—that they either found or created for themselves. From a fort made out of blankets to a special limb in a tree to a place behind the garage to a playhouse, indoors or out, it was a place where we felt cherished and safe. It was a place that spoke to us in a silent language and that will still speak to us if we let it.

In her mid-seventies, Rosemary left her abusive and alcoholic husband after 50 years of marriage, bought a small house, and began to live the rest of her life by herself. She had never lived alone before. Growing up she was the oldest of 13 children and was always babysitting and caring for kids. Her room often housed two or three other siblings at any one time. If she ever had a room to herself, she never remembered it.

Her parents moved their large family to a bigger place when Rosemary was about 11 or 12. Babies were still arriving and they needed more bedrooms. Shortly after moving in, she discovered a small but workable room under the basement stairs. It had evidently been a fruit cellar at one point, with a light and some shelving, but it wasn't being used now. Rosemary claimed it. She put a small cot in there, a little lamp, filled the shelves with some books and pictures, shut the door and for the first time found that she could be alone.

One day after school she came home to discover that her father had painted the entire basement a dull khaki color, including her room. In Rosemary's eyes, her little space had been exponentially enhanced. She would often sit in her room with the door locked, soaking up the privacy. It didn't release her from enormous babysitting duties, but it did give her moments to imagine another kind of life for herself and it did give her a chance to feel as though she had a place in the world. She recalled how she would sit on her little bed, look around, and say "I'm the luckiest little girl alive!"

Sixty some years later when Rosemary moved into her home, the first thing she did was paint her bedroom a dull khaki color, much to the horror of her grown children. That hadn't been her intention when she went to the paint store to pick out a color for her bedroom walls, but when she saw it, there was no question in her mind. Rosemary knew she had to remember how it felt to be the luckiest little girl alive, particularly as she healed from a marriage of heartache and abuse.

It's important to reflect on what kind of place you created as a child, not only to recapture those fond memories, but also to see if you have subconsciously created it in your current home. Perhaps you've duplicated some of the physical aspects of your secret place—it's outside, or it's in a basement, or the attic, or you used a similar color. Maybe it isn't duplicated in any physical ways but instead you've captured the feeling you got from your childhood place—where for a time you felt important, you felt safe, you felt in control.

The importance in remembering your childhood place is not to make you a child again, but to help you find your inner child. It is that inner child within you that dreams and creates, imagines and loves. At one time, you had a physical place that spoke to you of these things, and it will speak again if you can remember how to listen. If recreating it or any of its aspects physically is not possible, you may need to access your secret place through your imagination. This will allow you to manipulate and change the features easily and effortlessly until you've captured exactly the look and feel you want.

> Inventories from children's hiding places and from religious holy places bear remarkable similarity.
> —*Ordinarily Sacred,* Lynda Sexson

## Your Space as a Key to Who You Are

You can tell a lot about someone from being around their friends. You can also tell a lot about someone by being in their home. Just as good friends give each other feedback, your home can also provide some informative insights into who you are. Seeing the inside of someone's home is like a dip into their soul. I have had experiences when I've been unexpectedly surprised by what I had imagined I'd see and what I actually saw.

A middle-aged man asked me to come to his home because he was thinking of downsizing. I knew him through mutual friends and, from those casual meetings, had concluded he was a typical single guy. In my mind, this meant he would have hodge-podge furniture, artwork that consisted of unframed posters tacked onto the wall, and outdated carpet. Given the fact that all I had to go on were some brief conversations and my observation that he pretty much wore the same green sweater, my preconceptions couldn't have been more out of line.

When I got to his home, I encountered a man who had fine taste in French prints, who had shopped for months until he found a love seat that would fit perfectly in his living room, and had spent weeks sanding and sealing his beautiful hardwood floors all on his own. I realized I was seeing him in a new light, having been blinded by my own narrow assumptions. The next time I ran into him, I remembered the care he had given his home and how it had become a true expression of his soul. I looked at him differently and saw, not a "typical single guy," but an individual who was reserved, who had interests and dreams. My impressions made a complete turnaround because I got to see his home.

On the other hand, during my single days, I hung out with a friend who was the ultimate fashion-conscious gal. She never left her apartment without making some kind of style statement. Her hair was always in place, her purse matched her shoes, and her jewelry was carefully chosen to accent her outfit. Here again, I presumed this fastidious behavior carried over into her apartment. I was speechless when I picked her up one day to discover her place was in total upheaval. Clothes were everywhere and furniture was helter-skelter. She didn't have much of an explanation for the condition of her place but I understood why she had never invited me over. Just like my male friend, I saw her in a new light as well. Although her clothes may have provoked one kind of message, her home was in direct contradiction.

What I learned from these two experiences is that the true soul of someone is expressed through where they live. It's as though the curtains on the stage accidentally hit the floor enabling everyone else to get a glimpse of behind-the-scenes reality. Your space will not lie. It reflects the essence and the psychology of you and your home.

## Feedback from your home

Here is an exercise that can help you pull back the curtain on what your space says about you, both positively and negatively. More importantly, it helps you determine what qualities you find admirable and would consider worthy of incorporating into your own life. Conversely, you will come head-on with the negative qualities that you fear may become descriptors for you. The way you can access the information that your home holds about you is by doing a simple yet effective exercise using items from your space.

First, find one item in your home that you absolutely love— a piece of furniture, artwork, a rug, a wall color, fabric, etc. Write down one-word descriptors of that item—for example, unique, beautiful, elegant, etc. Write as many as you can, stopping only when you've run out of room on the paper or you've run out of appropriate words to describe the object.

Second, select something in your home that you hate or that just doesn't suit you (see any of the above for an example). Write down one-word descriptors of that item—for example, overbearing, cheap, outdated, doesn't fit, etc. Write down as many as you can.

Now, use the positive words to describe yourself: I am unique; I am beautiful, etc. One-by-one, go through all the words putting I am . . . in front of each of them. There is something inside you that vibrates to the qualities of the piece that you cherish. There's a resonance, an identification, a synergy—call it what you like—the item you love is mirroring something in you. Just as you and your friends typically have a lot in common and may even be described in similar terms, you have found a way to be reminded of the positive, cherished qualities in yourself.

Finally, use the words to describe what you hate or fear about yourself: I hate being worn out; I'm afraid I'm outdated, I hate that I'm broken, etc. You have now identified what features and qualities you do not like to see within yourself. These may be qualities you have dealt with in the past or are currently experiencing. They may be qualities you fear you may eventually take on.

Your space has given you some specific language that you can work with, both positive and negative. One can be your mantra (I am unique and beautiful and elegant) and can be repeated to yourself on an as-needed basis. The other phrases reflect what you do NOT want to be (I hate being broken, outdated, etc.). Obviously, you want to fill your space with items that support your positive mantra and you'll want to remove or change the items that support the negative one. This simple exercise opens your eyes to what your home may be saying to you and giving you clues as to who you truly are. Listen to the message you are getting from your environment.

The creation of homes reflects the ideals of
their owners.
  —*The Architecture of Happiness,* Alain deBotton

## Working at Home or Homing at Work?

Many people are working from home these days and enjoying
the experience. It is not only a time-saver in terms of commuting, but also an energy-saver in terms of fuel consumption. For
those starting a business, it is an inexpensive way to launch,
without having to incur outside rental costs. There may be
isolation issues for some people, but others find it a workable
and satisfying decision.

Rest assured your home also appreciates the experience
mainly because there's someone moving about the space,
there's activity and flow. The phone rings, the doorbell may
chime, people may visit—for your home, it beats sitting alone
day after day. However, there are some downfalls to working at home. This occurs when work starts to become the
main focus, overriding the protective, nurturing, entertaining
aspects of what a home is all about.

One of the issues with having your business in your home
has to do with boundaries—physical, time-based, and psychological. Some days it's nice to bring the laptop to the dining
room table and spread out—change of scenery is good. It
doesn't seem like a big deal to work a few hours in the evening
to get caught up on some projects. Furthermore, having your
office at home enables you to keep your nose to the grindstone,
available to anyone who is ready to offer some business day or
night. Caught up in the exuberance of starting a new business,
it's easy to jump in with both feet, devote hours and hours,

commit to projects, set aside personal obligations—all in the name of professional growth. Besides, initially it's so darn fun.

However, when the honeymoon phase starts to fade, it will seem like all you're doing is working. This is because you have set a standard that is hard to back away from. Working nights, weekends, spreading out all over the house, taking calls in the wee hours—it starts to feel and look as though you're living in your office. Your life gets out of balance.

It's not that a home office is a bad idea, but the business needs to have structure in order for you to find a sense of balance, poised between who you are at work and who you are in your personal life. In Feng Shui, we highly recommend that the office be contained in some way—in a room where the door can be closed or in a part of the house that is separate from your personal space. This gives you a physical as well as psychological message that you are in control of your space/life rather than the message that things have run amok.

Having a home office has the potential of splitting your focus when work things start to mingle with personal things. Finding a birthday card you meant to send to your uncle mixed in with a client's file or a business receipt in one of your cookbooks is a sign that boundaries are crossing. There's confusion, chaos, often culminating in a crisis. A business that is left to its own is a lot like having a new puppy. Until a system of confinement and discipline is in place, the business can scatter the energy of those who live there and the energy of your home.

Although a home prefers the activity of someone working there as opposed to being left alone day after day, it is not and was never intended to be a work place. I consulted with a young man who had bought a home and turned the whole place into an office. He left his house each morning and went to work—at another house. Bedrooms were set up as individual offices for employees, the dining room was the conference room, and the living room was his office. He was very proud of the makeover he had accomplished with this house-turned-business.

Although it seemed his business was initially very successful, there was arguably a disconnect between inside and outside, since it looked like a residence but inside it had an entirely different focus. In addition, there was a struggle between what the structure was intended to be when it was built and what it was trying to be now under different circumstances. So he not only had to deal with keeping his business afloat but he also had to manage the subtle tussle that was occurring within the walls. No surprise to me that, after a few years, his business failed and he had to sell the house as a foreclosed property. That's not to say I haven't seen many successful businesses being operated out of a home, but for the majority of them the enterprise was managed and contained.

## The Spirituality of Your Space

Perhaps the most poignant and meaningful influence your home can give you comes from its sacredness. Although the compass of our expectations is not pointed towards the discovery of holiness at home, this is where we can most easily create and access it. Everyday architecture can indeed provide a connection to your soul; it can renew your spirit and inspire you; it can be the vessel of reverence that you unconsciously reach for.

Whether growing up with a church, synagogue, or temple as a regular place of worship, it's not hard to define what a traditional sacred space looks like. Visiting cathedrals in Europe or Buddhist temples in China, there are certain unwritten criteria that seem to go along with a spiritually elevated place. We walk more slowly, we talk more quietly, and we often cover our heads. The space is clearly transformative, making it easy for anyone to move inward and take in the feeling and magnificence that are held within the walls.

Although you wouldn't want your home to duplicate this exact experience, there is a way to create a home that reenacts in a stepped-down version the lofty exaltation of a cathedral. According to Joseph Campbell, your home can become a sacred space when everything in it becomes symbolic— "mythologized," to use his word. In other words, it can feed your soul. It can become a prayer that is offered up on your behalf. Finding ways to intentionalize and spiritualize your space can result in a whole and holy home.

Returning to the Tao Te Jing statement that you can "know the whole world without leaving your home," your space is not only an arena of information but also a well of spirituality. If it's truly a sacred space, being at home would be revitalizing and renewing for your spirit and you would feel refreshed and balanced. The potential for tapping into the spirituality is profound and can be the ultimate reason you live where you do. Finding the inner sanctuary of your home, like finding your inner child, can open you up to the temple that you are along with a direct connection to your own destination.

Sacredness may be found in a specific place in your home. An obvious and common symbol of spirituality is an altar or an inspirational religious picture. People place special objects on their altar, all of which have meaning in some way—and all of which feel holy to them. A picture can offer the same experience whether it's of a saint, the Christ, Kuan Yin, Buddha, Gaia, a master, or something from nature. However, both of these options confine the sacred to one place or area. I propose that holiness is not limited by these physical reminders, although they are helpful, but instead can permeate and reflect out from the ordinary parts of your home as well.

Whether buying a rug, picking out a paint color, or selecting artwork, finding reverence is the argument for selecting only those things that inspire you. The word "inspiration" is derived from a combination of French and Latin words that means "taking in spirit." The question to ask is if that rug or that color or that piece of artwork lets you take in the essence of spirit. It's a different question than we would normally pose since our choices are usually driven by whether it matches the rest of the space or how much it costs or whether someone else will like it. Instead we should ask is: Will we be inspired by our selection? Will we be "spirit-ized" if we integrate it into our home?

As a Feng Shui consultant, too often I find someone in the family who has no place in their home to call their own. This is usually the female, but not always. She shares her bedroom with her spouse and her office with the kids. There is no one place she can designate as her place where she can be inspired, where she can find her soul. The sheer realization of this void often touches upon an ache that has never found conscious expression until that moment, but when brought to the surface brings with it some tears and determination to make a change.

A space that is sacred points toward reassurance and trust.

You can count on it. It makes you feel whole and safe. Nothing will harm you here if your space is truly holy. Whether this sacredness is confined to a room or a shelf, or even a corner, everyone needs a place that reflects to them the divine. When you're in the influence of your sacred space, you're infused with something beyond your own conscious mind and you find your strength and your clarity. You're inspired.

This sacredness occurs when the objects have your meaning and your intention as their driving force. Everything is chosen with care and has a common purpose—to lift you up spiritually. It doesn't mean you're striving for a Zen look nor does it mean everything has to be "in place" all the time. But when you're overwhelmed for whatever reason—work, relationships, money issues—then you have lost the sacred connection to your space.

Sometimes deliberately remembering the intentional parts of your space is enough to reconnect. Busy lives cause everyone to lose track of themselves. It may take only a moment to look around at the physical and symbolic sanctity to remember the divine. Sometimes sacredness can be reestablished in daily or weekly rituals. Call it Conscious Cleaning or Divine Dusting or Sacred Sweeping—a simple, common activity can not only uncover the sacred in the space, but can also have a spiritual component themselves.

An example of spiritual cleaning occurred years ago when I visited a church in a small English village, on my way to somewhere like Bath or Salisbury. I saw the spire as I approached the village so decided to check it out, plus it gave me an opportunity to get out of the car for a few moments. I went inside and took a seat in the back of the church. I was the only one there, until two women came through a side door with a bucket, rags, and a broom. For nearly 30 minutes I was mesmerized as I watched them carefully and quietly clean the church. One took the broom and gently worked her way through the rows of seats, straightening the hymnals and retrieving a couple of forgotten items.

The other worked at the altar, carefully wiping off the various statues and candles. She moved the items with reverence and precision. Sometimes she used a dampened cloth, other times she switched to a dry one. I'm sure she had a good reason for her procedure since it was clear to me this was not the first time either of these women had done this work. They didn't shout back and forth, but would walk over to the other and whisper if there was something to be said. I was mesmerized by their thoroughness and their patience. For a long time after that, I didn't vacuum without thinking about how those women would have done it. It caused me to slow down, be careful, and very intentional. It may have been my imagination but when I vacuumed in that way it felt like the carpet stayed cleaner longer.

In my opinion, if all homes were a reflection of spiritual sanctuary, we would easily move to world peace. Unfortunately, there's work still to do on this front so we all need to create holiness at home as our effort in the cause to create a whole global community.

## Your Home is Your Family

One of the definitions of the word family is "household." We maintain hope that our family, whether our family of origin or an extended one, will accept us as we are and encourage us on our path. We want them to be there for us through thick and thin, when we screw up and when we succeed. We want to rely on our family, not only for physical help, but more importantly for psychological support and for that unconditional presence which will never fail us.

The premise of *Conversations with Your Home* is that a home takes on an active and participative role in your life. It influences you, shapes you, guides you, and can lead you forward. Your home can help you reach back through the generations to bring forward your future. As Carl Jung said about his place in Zurich, it sustained his ancestors' souls, "since I answer for them the questions that their lives once left behind." It's as though your family lineage spans through the centuries and lives in your home with you—"as something forever coming into being and passing on." Your home holds that family trail just as it holds you.

Your home maintains the space for you to achieve wholeness and will maintain the symbol for that wholeness in ever-present ways, small or subtle ways, blatant and in-your-face ways. It will hold you until all the parts come together. A "house-hold" provides you the safety to search your heart. Your home can be your family with no exceptions or conditions. It is a place of ritual, of routine, and of reason. A "household" is your home's way of putting its arms around you and of protecting you. And that is its only purpose for being.

# *The Stages of Sanctuary*
## Exercises to Connect to Your Home

> To live in a sacred space is to live in a symbolic
> environment where spiritual life is possible,
> where everything around you speaks of the
> exaltation of the spirit.
>
> —Joseph Campbell

In line with the natural cycle of life, your home likewise goes through a parallel corresponding ebb and flow of energy. This section moves through five stages you and your house experience or may be experiencing together. Like any relationship, there are steps that take you from your first impression to your final goodbye. I've included stories in some of the segments that can further elucidate that particular phase—some stories from my own experience, some from my clients.

Along with the descriptions of each phase, you will find some relevant exercises to help you connect with your own home. You will want to read through the entire section first before actually doing any of the exercises, and then you can return to the ones that are most applicable to your situation. Some of them may not apply to you and your home; others will feel like a great fit. The goal is to become aware of what your space has to offer. It may take only one or two of the exercises or it may take several of them before you uncover the relationship and find the essence of your home.

The first stage is about Purpose and includes the initial steps to take with a new home—new to you or a newly-built space. The first section, Claiming Your Home, is appropriate when you first move into a space, whether purchased or a rental. There is also a section on Building Your Home for those who have the opportunity to find the appropriate land and be witness to the construction of the house. The last section is Finding One Another which underscores the importance of hearing the call from a home that may entice you with the purpose of learning a valuable lesson.

The second stage is about Progression and covers some actions that you can take to get to know your home in a more intimate way. Naming your home and determining the gender of your house, two possible ways to do this, are found in the section called Making Friends. Sharing Dreams walks through the steps of writing a letter to your home.

Passion is the focus of the third stage and includes three sections that take your relationship to a more in-depth level. Stayin' Alive points out ways to keep your home vital, current, and alive. An Ailing House addresses issues that could cause a home to become sick and how your gratitude can make the difference. Finally, Making the House Something It Isn't gets you in touch with the true spirit of your home while seeing it in a more objective way.

The Protection stage is appropriate for a discussion of death. The section Death at the Door covers the role a house will play when someone who lives there is dying. The section, Does a House Die? exemplifies the resilience of a space and how it responds to someone's efforts to revive it. This section culminates with an exercise where you prompt your home to speak to you in a letter.

The last stage is about Parting. The section on Losing Your Home discusses how to memorialize a space you once called home and, for whatever reason, is no longer yours. Movin' On illustrates how a home understands the appropriate time for you to leave and helps you to do that.

Making a connection with your home is refined and delicate work. Don't be discouraged if, after doing some of these exercises, you feel as though "nothing is happening" or that "it isn't working." Your home appreciates any gesture toward an interaction and will wait while you discover the best way for you to find one another.

A house that has been experienced is not an inert
box. Inhabited space transcends geometrical space.
—*Poetics of Space,* Gaston Bachelard

# Purpose

## Claiming your home

Whether you've been living in your home for years or have
just moved in, a simple ritual that involves an official transfer
of ownership is appropriate and thoughtful. For many people
"claiming their home" means they received papers that say the
house is now theirs or they have a lease that says they can live
there for a certain amount of time. That's one way.

A more meaningful way to lay claim to your property is to
make an intentional gesture that clears the energy. This clearing may be from prior occupants and their corresponding
experiences or it may be from challenging moments that have
occurred while you are living in the home—everything from
arguments, abuse, or the death of someone. These negative
influences can and should be cleared out. It not only enables you
to "start again" without remnants of past disturbances, but it is
also a blatant commitment about taking ownership of the home.

As a general rule of thumb, it is a good idea to reclaim and
reclear the space on a regular basis, much like cleaning the
house. How often you do it depends on what may be taking
place. There may be phases when life is progressing smoothly
and you don't feel the need to do anything. Clearing and
claiming once a year may be more than sufficient. But if you
have been faced with difficulties on what seems to be an ongoing basis, it may be appropriate to come up with some way to
"start again" on a more frequent timeframe.

## Claiming your home

### 1. Object
Select incense, a candle, a bell, a statue or picture of a deity, or anything else that seems powerful to you and will help you facilitate a change in the energy of your home.

### 2. Open windows and doors
Open as many windows as possible (at least one in each room) and all outside doors which symbolically draws out any stagnant air or negative energy.

### 3. Start at front door
Take the incense or candle or whatever object you have chosen to use, stand inside the front door, facing into your home. Hold the object in front of you as though you are "presenting" it to your house.

### 4. Move through your home
Going clockwise or counter-clockwise doesn't matter, just keep moving. See the object you're holding acting like a leaf blower, moving negative energy out. Imagine the difficult and painful memories of past or even current events being driven out through the nearest doors and windows.

Go in the basement, the attic if possible, closets, even rooms you don't use much.

### 5. Return to front door
When you've walked through your whole house, return to the front door. Place the object near the front entry for a few days to act as a temporary protector.

### 6. Be grateful
As you walk around closing windows and shutting doors, sense the bright and new energy in all the corners. Say thank you silently or aloud in each room.

## Building your home
If you are in the process of building your home, this is a great time to infuse the space with your own and your family's intentions. It is also the perfect time to uncover the kind of energy the house is bringing with it. The earlier this process can get underway, the better. In fact, it's best to start before the house has even started to take form.

Walking the property helps you as future occupants claim the real estate in more ways than just through a purchase agreement. It also provides an opportunity to "read" the land without the influence of the structure. Getting acquainted with the topography and the trees can give you the chance to anticipate features and to visualize how the house will fit. By doing this, you will also be able to predict things like the view from the bedroom window, which trees will provide shade, and where the swing should go. It helps you establish a familiar sense of "home" before there even is one.

Try to make these land visits as often as possible. You will get used to the roads that take you to your new place; you integrate the route into your driving pattern and you may even find a shortcut. Kinesthetically, your body finds its way home. Meanwhile, you may also locate grocery stores and drug stores, the post office and the nearest veterinarian—convenient services that are part of a typical lifestyle.

On sunny, warm days, why not bring a picnic and have lunch where the kitchen will eventually be? Or why not sit on the ground and talk where the family room soon will be located? In a relaxed, receptive state, you may get a multitude of ideas about what your life is going to be like. You may well get information from the land and from the future home that could determine some of your site decisions and your design choices.

My husband shared with me that as a young man he had the opportunity to build a home from scratch. He purchased the land and spent six months designing and planning the house. He enjoyed many hours on the land, imagining the house in various spots, checking the tree locations, and considering the sun's position. He became so connected to the space that he even dreamed about his new home.

The day after the contractor dug the foundation, my husband paid another visit to the land and, as he was walking toward the property, "saw" his house in completed form right in front of his eyes. Seeing the energetic outline of his dream house made him understand that already it was alive and had its own presence, even though it hadn't been built yet. He always loved that home and to this day speaks of it fondly, even though circumstances required him to move away after only a few enjoyable years.

*Diane's story*
My husband and I bought a piece of land about 10 years ago. We connected with it in many different ways. When we first started going to the land, we went in with a little hand held compass and a hatchet. It was densely wooded and we needed to make a pathway. We really wanted to know our land so we

walked it, and walked it, and walked it, and then walked it some more. We walked the perimeter and marked our boundaries. (I amazed my husband with my great compass skills thanks to my dad!)

We found a nice clearing in the middle of the south sector—it had an open pond right in the middle of a meadow. Woods and hills were to the north—how perfect it all felt. About half way up our hill is a level spot of ledge rock (the first place my husband kissed me on the land—thereafter called "The Kissing Rock").

As the years have passed, we now have many little paths through and around our land. A little cabin was built in a tucked-away clearing close to the meadow. To this day, as we walk our land we find rocks—some big and some small. If they are heart-shaped, we put them on the Kissing Rock—it's become an altar. If we had not taken the time to know our land, feel the space and let the land speak to us, we would not have the happy memories we have nor would we have found that perfect spot for our future retirement home.

Being actively involved in the birth of a home could be an appropriate time to determine its name. I worked with a family who came up with five names they thought the house would like. During their visits to the property, they would "try on" the names to see if any one felt just right. I encouraged them to also be open to the possibility that the house may one day unexpectedly present its name in their minds—a name that may not be on their list, which is exactly what happened in this case. The names they were considering were names of planets (Venus, Mars, Mercury, etc.) One day, one of the children came up with the name Amore—everyone loved it and decided that was perfect.

*More about naming your home can be found on page 80, Exercise: Naming your home.*

The gender of the house might also become apparent which could obviously influence a name choice. For some of my clients, they just know whether they're dealing with a male or a female house. They don't know how they know this—they just do. They'll say things like, "The roof is on. He's coming right along." Or, "She's a beauty—we can't wait to move in." Like picking a name, determining the gender is an action that comes from the heart.

*Find out more about determining the gender of your home on page 74, Exercise: Determining the gender of your home.*

Throughout the entire construction process, it is important for you to make appearances onsite as often as possible. Not only to determine if the house is being built according to specifications but also to reinforce and build up familiarity with the land and the structure. When it comes time to move in, these frequent visits will make it seem as though you are truly "coming home" since everything will be recognizable, identifiable, and expected.

Once the ground has been broken, you have a once-in-a-lifetime chance to relate to your home in a basic and raw state. There are various steps that can be taken during the construction process that can help you claim your new home and that can be an invitation for your home to get involved as well.

## Building your home

You may not be able to get onsite for each and every step as outlined below, but attempt to do as many as you can. The best time of day to visit is after the construction crew has vacated the area—not only for your own sense of privacy but also, practically speaking, so you don't get in the way of their work.

1. Foundation has been dug
Sprinkle uncooked rice into the foundation where your home will be built, walking the perimeter as you do. Rice holds an intention about growing new possibilities and a new life. Placing it under the foundation of your home means those intentions will be infusing the structure from the bottom up.

2. Foundation blocks in place
If financial stability is a concern or you anticipate it could be a concern in the future, place money inside the actual foundation blocks in the four corners of what will become the home. This doesn't have to be a lot of money—pennies even—although I encourage you to implement ways to make the coins special. Place either 3 or 9 coins in each corner because these are important numbers in Chinese philosophy.

Three is based on their fundamental belief that the universe is comprised of heaven, earth, and humanity. Nine is obviously three times three, plus it's the largest yang number so holds some extra power. You might place coins that were minted in a special year—the year you were born, the year you got married, the current year, etc. Although this isn't a huge money investment, the intention is focused on financial wholeness. But, just for a moment, think about placing a one hundred dollar bill in each corner. The house would certainly be ramped up with a strong statement about being abundant—plus you would never forget that they were tucked in the corner somewhere!

3. Sheet rock phase

Place pictures of the people who will be living in the house in an envelope and slip it in the wall near your front door.

Write out sayings that are especially inspiring to you and your family and place in a wall in an appropriate part of the home. For example, if you particularly like an inspirational message that applies to your work, write it on a piece of paper and place it in the wall of your future office. If you have a saying or prayer that relates to healthy eating, write it down and place it in one of the walls of what will be the kitchen.

If you have a special stone or a crystal, you may want to place that near the center of your house so it can radiate in all directions and positively impact countless parts of the space—and your subsequent life.

These items stay where they were placed until the house is no longer standing, so priceless, precious gems —or even hundred dollar bills—may not be a good choice if you're counting on retrieving them at some point. The purpose isn't about getting them back anyway; it's about giving your home a hint as to what you want to create in this space. As the home forms itself around you and your family, the objects will be a reminder about what is important to you. Plus, you can look back on the days or moments when you intentionally placed the picture or the coins or stone in the structure of your home. You can visualize them in the wall or behind some sheetrock, quietly holding a dream you expressed for yourself and for your family, knowing you are being protected and embraced with your unique blueprint.

## Finding one another

Accustomed as you are to providing for your home, taking it on as a responsibility, being diligent about keeping it in good working order, you may be overlooking the possibility that the house may actually be taking *you* on as a responsibility and is trying to keep *you* in good working order. When something breaks down or stops working at home, perhaps it's due to frustration and exasperation in trying to keep you on your path. Is it possible your home is expressing fatigue or trying in any way that it can to get you to pay attention to the message? Rather than becoming irritated about this breakdown, maybe a better approach would be to look at what about your own life needs fixing, no matter what the price.

Bernie and Ruth invited me to look at a house they were proposing to buy. They were so excited about it. Bernie loved the double garage and the large garden in the back. Ruth knew that under all the paint there was beautiful oak woodwork and couldn't wait to uncover it. The house had a charm from the early 1900s which spoke to them. I could see it needed a lot of work, but they couldn't wait to start their lives in this place. From a Feng Shui perspective it had integrity, so I had no reason to discourage their decision, even if I could.

A year later, Ruth called me. They hated the house. They would have put it back on the market, but it was in such a mess that it would never sell. They asked me to pay them a visit. In their enthusiasm, they had begun remodel projects in every room. Bernie had also rented a back-hoe and dug up the back yard to work on the garden, but never got around to planting anything. Everywhere they looked, there were unfinished projects. They had reached their limit. Any enthusiasm and excitement I saw during my initial visit was gone.

So we sat and talked about what happened. The first few months after they moved in, they had excitedly forged ahead with remodel/repair ideas with no plan in mind. When they got tired of working in one area, they started on another. Eventually, everything was torn up. They ate on cardboard boxes and slept in sleeping bags—not where they thought they would be one year after purchasing the house. I helped them prioritize their projects and strongly recommended they stay in one area before moving on. I had them begin in their master bedroom. They assured me they were open to finding another way and appreciated the insight about focusing.

Within five to six months, Bernie and Ruth had pretty much completed their house remodel. When I returned to look at the results, this is when I knew the house had lured them in for a reason. The home was spectacular. They both realized it had indeed become a lovely place in which to live. I could even catch some of their original excitement by the way they talked about their home now. They had learned some lessons about focusing and patience which, they were the first to admit, had carried over into other parts of their lives.

Because of the unexpected tutorial from the house, Bernie shared he recognized a similar behavior in his job, which was not serving him well. He would start one project at work and then jump to another before wrapping up the first one. Seeing the disarray in his house was all too familiar. As he began to concentrate on projects at home, he correspondingly found himself concentrating on his job responsibilities in a more sequential manner, completing one before launching into something new. The house had certainly done a good job of calling in the right people to not only learn a thing or two about focus but also to uncover its own latent beauty.

It is no accident you're in the home you're in. In most cases, you made a conscious decision to select a particular house. There was something about the space that attracted you and lured you into its walls. I always ask people what it was about the space that they originally loved. Why, from all the other homes/apartments/condos they could have chosen, why did they choose this one? At this point, most people smile. There's something about remembering the excitement of having found the "right" house for them that brings about a positive reaction. The reasons for selecting a particular space are as varied as the types of homes available: I adored the porch, I fell in love with the kitchen, it's close to school, it's close to the freeway, it's far away from my parents, it had a wine cellar. There may have been many reasons why you chose the house you're in, not just one. Although you may forget what exactly caught your eye, remembering those first impressions can be helpful and insightful. It brings you back to the beginning, where the relationship with your space began.

It is also possible that after a few years, you may feel like you made a mistake by moving into this particular home. Things aren't going all that well in your life and the house doesn't seem to be performing the way you want. There have been repairs and expenses you hadn't counted on. You've had to make sacrifices in order to keep the house working properly. You figure that perhaps if you moved, things would get better. You could start over somewhere else and forget about this place.

Unfortunately, I've seen clients pack up and leave a troublesome home only to move into another one that turned out to be even more of a challenge. We not only take our problems with us but, in the act of moving, those challenges seem to magnify. Of course, an argument could be made that someone else chose the house for you and you never wanted it from the beginning or, due to timing, you felt you had no choice in the matter and had to purchase the first thing that came along. This doesn't justify moving out of the home. Regardless of the circumstances of why you're in the space, the space has something to teach you and you're there for a reason.

A space will draw in people who have the potential to learn from the home and who, in turn, have the potential to care for the home in a specific way. The buyers may not know that going in, but the house sees them capable of making things right. If a house has been abandoned or is in need of a lot of repairs, someone could likely be lured in by a totally unrelated aspect (I loved the porch, it's close to work, etc). The dilemma comes when people move in and afterwards realize all that will be required of them. For some reason they didn't see it prior to their purchase, or chose not to see it.

They feel betrayed by the house, expecting one set of circumstances but encountering another less desirable set. However, here is where the value comes in—here is where the lesson is learned. Here is where they must stay, until they have completed their work with the house.

I've worked with several clients who moved into what they thought was their dream home only to discover there were entities in various parts of the space. In all these cases, the occupants were familiar with the importance of releasing these spirits and set about doing so with unswerving determination. In a few cases, the owners did it themselves. Others found the right people to handle the situation. In either case, the house was restored to a peaceful environment, devoid of the disruption caused by a confused and lost soul. It was no accident those particular individuals were drawn into the space.

Over a period of a few years I consulted with a number of people who had recently moved only to find out after moving in that their homes had experienced some kind of trauma in prior years. In one case the house had had a fire a few years earlier. Abusive behavior was revealed in another home. A different client found out from the neighbors that someone had been murdered in their new home. In these situations, the owners took the responsibility for making things right, through rituals, blessings, or remodeling certain areas. The occupants hadn't budgeted the time or money to heal such wounds, but felt it was the right thing to do. It's as though during the initial "courting" stages, a space put its best foot forward to make a good impression on the person or people who can and will eventually diminish the effects of such traumas.

Sometimes, however, the buyer will feel like they've made a huge mistake moving into the space and look for ways to get out. I recently read about a couple who bought and moved into a home in our neighborhood and then found out from the neighbors that the previous owner had been murdered in the house. They were furious and were trying to sue the real estate agency to get their money back. They were sure they heard the dead person in their basement and couldn't sleep. In fact, they had closed up the house and moved to a hotel until this could all get sorted out. I drove by the house to see what it looked like. My heart ached for the space which was now abandoned with shades drawn down and flyers piling up by the front door. It was a very attractive home but surrounded by impenetrable sorrow. I have no doubt the new buyers had the ability to heal the space, to bring it back to health and wholeness. But somehow the line of communication wasn't clear between them and their home and they ran.

A house can entice someone to move in because it's lonely. The previous occupants travelled a lot, or lived elsewhere for half the year, or simply didn't get around to fixing anything. Without fail the next owners who are attracted to the house will have children, they might work out of the house, they may entertain regularly. The house sees to it that the energy of the new people will often fulfill what was lacking in the prior ones.

Generally, dwellings do not like to be rented. It's rare when the owner of a rental truly cares about the space itself. Most rental property is acquired as a financial investment. Tenants never forget they don't own the walls so they will adopt a "who cares" attitude. Broken things don't get fixed because there's no investment by the occupant or the absentee owner. "It's not my place so I'm not going to bother," says one party. "I don't live there so I won't worry about it," says the other. A space desperately tries to bring in someone who will commit. I've been in homes that had been rental properties for years and years and were now being occupied by owners. There's nothing like the reawakened hum that comes from a space that is being reclaimed and cared for after years of neglect.

Homes don't just call in someone to make repairs and get them looking better. A well-balanced home may attract someone in to help the occupants heal. They may tempt a person to move in because that particular home knows how to help the new occupant in a specific way. Whether from a physical illness, a mental struggle, or some emotional upheaval, a home can offer support and comfort. A home could be a perfect setting for success in business and will, of course, look for someone to match that quality. A house can also teach us hard things—like patience when the furnace keeps acting up. Or it can teach us about being mindful of our actions as we catch ourselves from falling down the steps to the basement because we were preoccupied. It can teach us about loss and forgiveness when our things are brutally lost in a fire or theft, flood, or a tornado. It can teach us about staying focused as Bernie and Ruth's house did.

Houses can teach us things that we may not be learning anywhere else. They can teach us about security and feeling safe. They can hold our family together during tough times and joyous occasions. They can comfort us. After a long absence, many of us walk in the front door and say, "It's so good to be home." I can only imagine how a house must feel when it hears those words.

A house has a way of luring in the "right" buyers at the right time. The timing may be crucial for the people or it may be crucial for the home, or a little of both. Either way there is a very important reason the two have come together.

*TR's story*
In May 1998 I decided the time seemed right to buy my first home. I got my financing in order and found a great real estate agent. By mid-June we had looked at a few homes. It was a sellers' market and bidding wars were fierce. I had already lost one home (in hindsight, I'm glad) when my agent called to say a home that met my parameters was going on the market that afternoon. We set up a 4:45 PM appointment.

I pulled up in front at 4:30 PM and knew it was my home.

She virtually spoke to me. Another party was looking at the house with their realtor, so while I waited in the car I kept thinking: This is my house—you don't want it—go away. When my agent got there, I ran over to her car and said: This is my house—we don't have to go in—let's make an offer. Of course we went in, but everything I saw confirmed that it was indeed mine. We made an offer that evening and it was accepted. Later I found out that three other people had also made an offer, but they accepted mine even though I don't think it was the highest bid.

My house and I have been happy together ever since. Each day before I leave for work, I tell the animals to be good and to take care of each other. I tell the house to take care of the animals as well, that I love them all, and when I expect to return. Every day they do take care of each other.

**Recalling your first impression**
This exercise is intended for you to remember what you loved about your home when you first saw it. If you moved into a place that you did not personally choose (someone else bought it or was living in it when you moved in), then see if there was a feature of the house that you appreciated at that time.

I. Recollecting your memories
Move back in time to when you first laid eyes on the space in which you're living. Relive the moment when you first walked up to the front entry and recapture your feelings.

2. Determine that special thing
Ask yourself what it was that captured your heart (hardwood

floors, beautiful kitchen, charming garden, fond memories, etc.) or what captured your mind (affordable, your partner lives there, close to work, close to school, etc.).

3. Is it still special?
Determine if you're still charmed by that feature or whether it no longer holds the importance it did in the beginning. Has the feature, in fact, become the opposite for you—a detriment, and you may be asking yourself why you ever were enamored with that feature at all.

4. Capture the experience
Write in a journal or your house scrapbook what the feature was—maybe you have pictures of it or can draw it—describe what it was and how you felt about it. Then document how you feel about it now and whether you would use that same feature for your next home.

This exercise can not only help you remember a potentially fond moment between you and your home, but also can help clarify your feelings in general about where you're living. You could do this exercise with other homes you've lived in to see if you've consistently been attracted by the same features.

If you moved into a space because of circumstances, depriving you of the opportunity to choose it yourself, think about what has become special to you now about this place. If nothing about your home is special to you, ask yourself if there are small areas that could be made special. If you claimed a room or a corner or a shelf, ask your heart if it's possible to create something distinctive and unique that would provide you fond memories after you no longer live there.

# Progression

## Making friends

Years ago, I lived in England in a small cottage in the countryside just outside of Oxford. I had noticed a small sign by the driveway with the words "Linden Lea" written on it, but I could hardly make out the lettering and it was close to falling apart. I was going to remove it and throw it in the garage but never got around to it.

One day I realized that, although I had been living there for some time, I hadn't been receiving any mail. This didn't seem right knowing my family and friends. So I went to the "post" to see if I could sort it out. We were living in a very small village where the post office was part of the general grocery store.

The postman assured me there was no mail under my name. I stood there with a puzzled look, wondering if perhaps a stack might have been misplaced somewhere. He looked around again, even went in a backroom, which was more like a closet. He came back empty handed. My disappointment must have been evident as he happened to ask where I was living. I gave him the street address, but he wanted the NAME of my cottage. I told him about the sign with "Linden Lea" on it and he lit up. Yes, indeed, there was mail for me. All of it had been filed under the house's name, not mine. The postman, for whatever reason, thought the cottage was vacant so instead of leaving mail at an empty place, he took note of the name on the sign and brought it back to the post office each day, assuming at some point someone would come to claim it. Once my friends and relatives addressed the envelope with the name of the cottage, there were no further problems.

In England, as in many part of Europe, homes had names, particularly when they lived in small villages like the one we were in. And, as I found out, the name took precedence over the occupant and the street or road address. There was always a reason for the particular name of the space, too. Our cottage was called Linden Lea because it was sited on a field of linden trees. Our neighbors' house was called "The Old Bakery" for obvious reasons. Further down the road, another house was called "Creek's End"—no creek but perhaps that's how the house got its name.

As a Feng Shui consultant, I often address the issue of people who live in a space that has no meaning for them. This situation can come about in many ways. Sometimes a person moved into a house a long time ago and now they no longer like the house, yet are not financially in a position to move. Sometimes a person has been left behind as the result of a divorce, living with constant reminders of the battlefield the space once was. Sometimes a person just moved into a home based on a great first impression, only to find that the house is requiring a lot of them, energetically and financially. One of the hardest situations is when someone moves into a partner's home, especially if the partner has lived there a long time and particularly if the partner had previously lived there with someone else.

In all cases, someone is living in a space that doesn't seem to be working in their best interests and moving is out of the question. They call me looking for a way to make the best of a tough situation.

I suggest they "name" their house. Although this idea may evoke some surprise and hesitation, my point is to help them establish a personal bond with the space in order to allevi-ate some of the alienation. A name will help personalize the association; the act of naming it enables a person to claim it. There's a sense of ownership with something that is named. It's odd not to name a pet and lots of people name their cars. So why would naming your house be any different?

Nevertheless, we're not accustomed to naming houses. Although initially it may sound like a strange exercise, it can actually bring about amazing changes. Once you've named your house, you're more likely to have compassion and patience around any trouble that might come up. It's less likely that you'd cut corners when doing repairs or cleaning if the space has an identity to you. In a space that's been difficult for a person, calling it by name shifts the association completely. The space has become special.

One way to determine a name, is to ask yourself what changes you would like to initiate in your life. One of my clients who wanted additional prosperity decided to name his space Prospero, a play on the word "prosperity." A woman of Italian heritage who wanted to increase her wealth named her home Lira, the original currency of Italy. Ben was the chosen name for a house owned by a young couple who wanted to attract lots of one hundred dollar bills (Benjamin Franklin's picture is on a one hundred dollar bill).

Another way to find a name is to express a theme such as Joy, Hope or Friendship. An elderly woman who did, in fact, name her house Amiga (Spanish for female friend) found that, shortly after doing so, her space became the meeting place for her friends. They cooked meals at her house and gathered for birthdays, celebrations, etc. When looking for a space in which to hold meetings for their book club, it was unanimous that Amiga was the perfect spot. It should be obvious that naming your home Moldy or Money Pit will not serve the best interest of the relationship between you and your home. The intention is to try to ease a challenging and difficult situation, not magnify it.

Before considering a name, it may be helpful to determine if there's a gender attached to your house before naming it. Some spaces are definitely more feminine, while others project a more masculine feeling. This factor could influence a particular name for your home.

If it feels important to determine whether your house is male or female, there are some indicators that may help you decide. You may just have a knowingness about its gender, or a gender-specific name for your home may have already come to mind. Something like "Gabriel" or "Evangeline" is a pretty clear indicator whether a space is male or female. My experience has been that, like ships, a lot of homes tend to be female. However, you shouldn't rule out the distinct possibility that yours may be an exception to that observation.

**Determining the gender of your home**
Here are some ways to help you determine the gender of your home:

1. Shape of house:
If the right side of your home (determined by standing in your front doorway and looking out to the street) is larger or more pronounced in some way, then there is a lot of female energy in the space.

If the left side is more prominent, then it is a male house.

## Examples of a female home

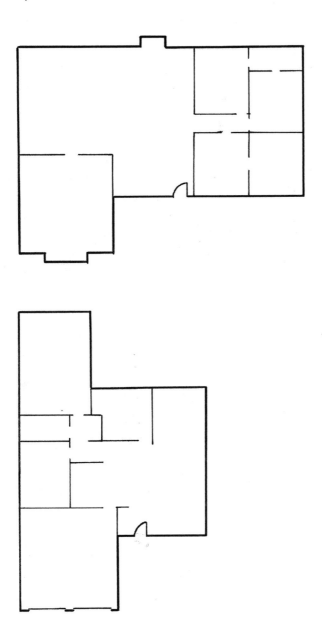

## Examples of a male home

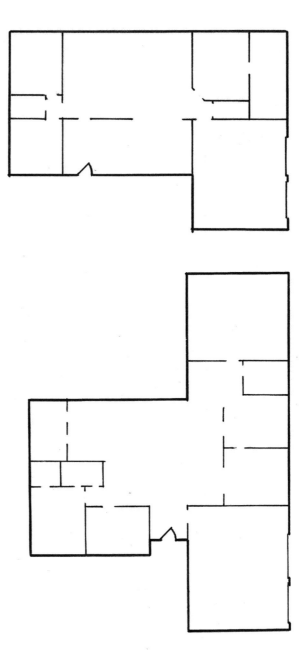

If your house is evenly proportioned, then you will have to determine the gender in other ways.

2. Address numbers
The sum of your house numbers can determine gender. Add up the individual numbers of the house until you get to a single digit. Refer to chart for gender indication.
(Ex.: House is 17436 W. Main Street.
Add 1 + 7 + 4 + 3 + 6 = 21; 2 + 1 = 3; 3 is a male number)

| | |
|---|---|
| 1 – male | 6 – male |
| 2 – female | 7 – female |
| 3 – male | 8 – male |
| 4 – female | 9 – female |
| 5 – can be either male or female | |

3. Year the house was built
Add up the numbers of the year the construction was completed on your house. Then refer to chart above.
(Ex.: House completed in 1945.
Add 1 + 9 + 4 + 5 = 19; 1 + 9 = 10; 1 + 0 = 1;
1 is a male number).

4. Direction of house
Determine the direction the house faces and refer to chart for gender orientation.
(Ex.: If you house faces northwest, that direction is male energy).

| | |
|---|---|
| North – male | Northwest – male |
| Southwest – female | West – female |
| East – male | Northeast – male |
| Southeast – female | South – female |

You may want to determine the gender of your home by doing all four steps. If you obtain the same gender on the majority of the steps, then you have discovered which orientation your home prefers. If it's an even split, then you will have to rely on your own intuition or on what name may be appealing to you to uncover the gender.

Consider carefully what you select for a name or title because it may bring what you are unconsciously asking for. A female client named her apartment Clare, a name with no special association, just one she always liked. She hadn't lived there four months before she received "clare"-ity around her job (which she quit) and a relationship (which she dumped). Although all changes that she did not regret, she was not as prepared for them as she would have liked. Naming their lake home Hanson's Inn, a retired couple was overrun with constant visitors. Their guests would remark on what a wonderful place it was and how comfortable they felt when they were there. The owners felt like they were running a hotel. It wasn't until they changed the name to Hanson's Haven that things started to quiet down for them.

I didn't realize one of my students had named her little house Faith until later in our relationship. I always heard her say "I have faith," but thought it was merely her way of expressing a belief in cosmic order. She was actually saying "I have Faith" meaning she had a place to call her own; everything would be all right.

A young man named Pete hired me to come to his new condominium.

He had bought it, knowing it was a good investment for him, but something didn't feel right. He couldn't put his finger on the problem, but he felt isolated, alone and vulnerable. He also shared with me that right before he moved in he had to put his dog to sleep due to a long and dreadful illness. He got tears in his eyes even as he spoke about it with me. Mack had been his dog as a kid; after college they were inseparable. Part of Pete's loneliness in his new place was living without his best pal. He decided to name his place Mack in memory of his friend. Doing so honored his dog as well as shifted his feelings of isolation.

A name can be made up of a derivative of a virtue, like Serenity or Joy or Hope. It's common to have two names but not necessary—Peaceful Pad, Cozy Corner. You may even want to combine your name with another descriptor, like Sarah's Sanctuary, Terry's Tree House, or The Nelson's Nest. You could name your home after a place you've visited or would like to visit—Glengarry, Shanghai, Birmingham. There may be an aspect of nature you'd like to capture: field, meadow, lane, plantation, forest, woods.

You could also use your house to call in some aspect that you want, but currently don't have. This is particularly helpful for those people who are struggling with their home. A home that has had a lot of repairs and expenses may do well with a name using the word Whole or Wholeness. If you've experienced a lot of financial issues while living in your space, consider using a name Fortune or Fortunate, Rich or Blessing, to help turn things around. If you're looking for a relationship, a name with Loving, Love, or Heart as part of its title will solidify its intention.

Whether you're not enjoying the experience of the house you're living in or whether you have found it to be a blessing in your life, naming your home may be a gift you give to both of you.

Like naming a child, it is important to give your house a name that you find pleasant and appropriate. You may never put the physical name blatantly on your door or on a sign in the front of the house, but your choice of a name can still be an important way to connect. Naming something means you have claimed it and made it your own.

## Naming your home

Follow these simple steps to arrive at a name you'd like to give to your house.

### 1. Get prepared

Prepare for this exercise by lighting a candle or turning the lights low. Grab a pad of paper and pencil along with 15–20 minutes of quiet time. Make sure you aren't going to be distracted. If you want to play some inspirational music or light some incense, feel free to incorporate these sensory options.

### 2. Move into the moment

Watch your breath gently going in and out. Bring the energy of the earth up into your heart and the energy of heaven down through the top of your head to also rest in your heart. Turn your attention to your home. Think about how it looks on the outside and the feeling you get when you walk inside. Let your thoughts meander to what this house has meant to you, both good and bad.

### 3. Find your center

Find the "center" of your home, whatever that might mean to you. It may be the physical center or a place where you can connect to the heart of your space. Move yourself into this spot in your mind.

## 4. Ask for a name
From your heart bring forth a request to your house for assistance in finding a name that best describes what it is here to do or represent. Ask for a word or phrase that would define and capture its dream and its alignment with yours.

## 5. Listen
Listen carefully to what your house whispers to you. Jot down ideas on your paper as they come. If you have already named your house, check in to see if it is still fitting, or if a name change is appropriate. Feel free to make suggestions and see how the house reacts.

## 6. Try it on
Once you've come up with a name, say it aloud or to yourself three times to see if it feels right to you and to your home. If not, go back to #4 and repeat.

## 7. Be grateful
When you've arrived at a name that you both feel is perfect, thank the house from your heart. Notice how you feel about your home now.

## 8. Anchor the name
Write the name of your home on a special piece of paper, fold it up, and put in a red envelope. Place it somewhere in a special area in your home—under a plant, under a rug, on an altar, or in a drawer. Be sure to put it in a place where it won't get lost or forgotten.

## 9. Use it
Use the name each day for nine days straight, either when coming in or going out.

Once you've determined a name, greet your house whenever you come in using its new name. Likewise, when you're leaving, let the space know your approximate return time, addressing it by name. This can be done silently if there's concern about reactions from other family members or roommates. However, you may certainly share the name with other family members if that feels appropriate. You can also do this exercise with your spouse or anyone else that lives in the home with you to determine a name everyone will appreciate.

I don't always suggest naming a house. But when I see an owner and their home struggling to be together, naming it is an energetic way to change their association. If at any time the name does not feel appropriate for whatever reason, repeat this exercise to secure a different one for your sanctuary.

My friend and writing buddy, Margaret, author of *Home— Inspired by Love and Beauty* is obviously very connected to her home. Despite the fact she and her husband had lived in their home many years and had found meaningful ways to make it a special haven, she had never considered naming their home. Due to the special bond she had with her house, she thought this exercise would be a meaningful one.

Before coming up with a name on her own, Margaret decided to engage her home in the process. One evening during a quiet relaxing moment, Margaret asked her home what name it would like to have. Almost instantly, she heard "Annabelle May." She couldn't imagine where this would be coming from as the name Annabelle had no meaning for her. No one in her family had that name, nor any of her friends. It had neither negative nor positive associations for her—the name simply appeared.

Later Margaret did a computer search for girls' names popular at the time her home was built (1920s). Annabelle was near the top of the list. So she "tried it on" for a few days and decided it was the perfect name for her family home.

It wasn't until after the naming incident that Margaret realized she had surrounded part of her home with several bushes of hydrangeas that seemed to thrive where nothing else would grow—the Annabelle variety.

### Sharing dreams

One night I woke up to some strange noises. They weren't all that loud, but loud enough that they disturbed my sleep. At first I figured my cats were playing around, but I soon discovered they were all sleeping soundly in various spots. So I tiptoed around to see if the doors were locked or if something had been knocked over. Everything seemed in perfect order. Then I heard it again.

I tried to determine where it was coming from but it was a fleeting sound, barely audible. I sat on the steps going back upstairs and waited for it to happen again. It didn't take long before I heard it once more. It was coming from nowhere but everywhere. I didn't know where to go to get closer to the sound as it was near me but coming from the other room. The sound came in irregular intervals—kind of a humming, coughing, snicker sound. It didn't frighten me but it was definitely coming from my house. After a while everything was quiet.

As I went back to bed, I remembered how I would watch one of my little cats make noises while she slept, dreaming about catching a mouse probably, and I wondered if my house was dreaming. Perhaps it was dreaming about a remodel project or about how hard it worked this winter to keep us warm. Maybe it was dreaming about playing with our cats, or about the recent group of students I had in our home.

I like to think houses only dream about happy things. They don't stay awake at night worrying about stuff, like the age of their shingles or the condition of the water heater. They don't dream about how clean their corners are. No, houses dream about joyful events and quiet, tender moments. They're at their best when they can hold an imprint of a spectacular occurrence—and that's what they dream about.

A few times since that night, I've heard those noises again. It's comforting to know the house feels confident about engaging in its own dreams. I love trying to figure out what might be on its mind, who or what is the catalyst for those little sounds. Maybe my house is remembering funny little stories about the cats or maybe it's dreaming about the back garden. Maybe my house is dreaming about me.

Aside from the obvious need to shelter and protect, houses are here for an express purpose. Some need to have children— lots of them, generations of children. Without the presence of children, the house doesn't stand as straight. On the other hand, some houses don't do well with children. I worked with a couple who were trying to conceive a child. The house had not had children within its walls ever before. After being in the house an hour or more, I was getting the clear message that the house was not open to the idea of children. It was a perfect home for adults and corresponding grownup activities, like dinner parties, political events, fundraising galas. It was clear to me no child would be born there. Unfortunately, it played out for them. A serious miscarriage put the wife in danger of ever conceiving again. Only after they moved to another place, did she easily and safely deliver a healthy baby.

A house's sole purpose might be a deliberate refuge. I once lived in a house that was built in such a way that it comfortably housed only me. People couldn't find me, I had trouble getting pizza delivered, and never had to buy candy for Halloween. But at that time in my life, I was fine with the invisibility. Trying to throw a party there or have people over was a challenge—parking was an issue, finding the front door was impossible without specific directions, the living room could only accommodate three to four people comfortably. I sold that property to a single man looking for a retreat—perfect.

On the other hand, there are homes that need to be entertainment sites, kids and all. The more people, the better. They love being the hub of activity. In fact, it would be a disservice to the home to move in and try to maintain a quiet, low-key life. Some homes dream about being a healing place and want to specialize in it. I worked with a client who had battled a chronic disease for years. The most relief she got was when she spent time on her enclosed back porch which overlooked a river. It provided a view of nature from a secure and safe vantage point. Years later when one of her dear friends was facing an arduous health crisis, my client invited her to come live at her house, more specifically spend time on the porch. A few months later, her friend moved back home, nearly recovered.

Houses have an innate dream to assist us in being the best that we can be. They want to infuse our aspirations and inspirations. More than anything a home dreams of connecting you to your roots and your inspiration—to your earth and your heaven. It acts as the transformer between two cosmic forces, blending their energy and presenting it to you in a way that you can receive, enabling you to fulfill your own dreams. It wants nothing more than to be that conduit, to help lift you up to your own insightful revelations.

Additionally, a home wants to reflect the dreams of its owners. It does that by expressing values we think are worthwhile. This expression makes us happy, for we often forget what our dreams were all about. We drift away from our true selves. So we depend on our homes to reflect the ideals we esteem and to provide us a template to bring us back to our vision. After a long, grueling day, we return home to our authentic self. Everything around us will prompt us as to our highest ideals and to our genuine heart. Although we may have temporarily let it slip from our memory, our home brings us face-to-face with our identity, a place of inspiration, integrity, and ingenuity. We can truly return home.

A wonderful way to share your dreams with your home is to write a letter to it. Each year on New Year's Day I write a letter to my house. It is a tradition that started shortly after moving in. In the annual letter, I thank it for all it did for us in the past year—the shelter, the comfort, the concern. It gives me a chance to outline our overall plans with regard to house and garden projects. I write about my dreams for the upcoming year. I list the activities I want to accomplish for myself and for my business. This list can range from "work out more" to "paint the closet in the basement."

I write about all the poignant things that have happened during the past year—the guests, the dinners, the holidays, happy news I processed at home and sad news. I reminisce about the quiet evenings, the fires in the fireplace, cat incidents, worried moments, and healing moments. It's not hard to feel the gratitude for having a place so tender and endearing with which we share our life.

Doing this exercise opens the door to answers, comments, and suggestions that might come from the house. Sometimes there's an immediate knowingness. One year I had just finished my house letter, bemoaning the fact that adding a solarium onto the back of the house just was not coming together. As I was signing off on my letter, I sensed confirmation that we were definitely on the wrong path with the solarium idea, that it was a much too extravagant plan. I "heard" that a deck would be perfect—an idea we had not considered. And it was . . . and is.

Another time we had been discussing how to reconfigure our upstairs rooms to expand a very small bathroom. I put the question to the house during the New Year's ritual. It wasn't until spring that I was hit with the answer. This one did require an extensive second-story addition onto the back of our house, but it's one which we've never regretted. On my own, I would never have tapped into that possibility.

I look forward to this annual conversation. It's exciting for me. The house opens up, shares ideas, and confirms for me that it is alive. During the course of the year, I regularly take counsel with my home, but it's typically about a specific issue. The year-end ritual, however, enables me and my home to look at the big picture. It gives us a chance to see if we still belong together, if we're still on compatible paths, if everyone's dreams are being fulfilled. As sad as that moment may be, I know there will be the day when the house may say to us it's time to start looking elsewhere for our place to live. For now, I feel like we've still got some years ahead of us, but I would never want to be presumptuous and ignore a gentle nudge from a place that has had nothing but our best interests at heart.

## Writing a letter to your home

You may want to have a house journal in which you keep a running log of the letters you write to your house. Or you can write these letters in your home's scrapbook. Either way, it will give you a chance to reread them over time. You may begin to see patterns arise in terms of issues. You may realize you've been grappling with the same problem for a very long time concerning your home or concerning your own life. By writing to your home regularly, you will find that your home is a ready participant in helping you attain your goals.

1. Gather writing implements
Plan to write in a journal that is specifically for the house or use the pages of the scrapbook you've devoted to your home. Or have paper and pen handy.

2. Quiet moment
Find a few moments of quiet time when you won't be disturbed and tune into the conscious spirit of your home.

3. Salutation
If you've named your home, you can start with
   Dear . . .
   Otherwise Dear Home is fine.

4. Complete the sentences
   What I love about you is . . .

My favorite time with you is . . .

I regret that . . .

Keep your thoughts related to your home. You may have regrets about other things in your life, but this sentence is to be directed to something you regret that refers directly to your home.

I'd like to change . . .

Again, keep it related to your home, not to things you want to change about yourself.

Thank you for . . .

You can thank it for the good things as well as the challenging things you have learned from your home.

5. Say goodbye
Express your intention to stay in touch, even if it's just

Talk to you later . . . and then sign your name.

There are no set rules as to how often you should write to your home, but I recommend that you write once a week in the beginning to break the ice. You may realize that after doing some other exercises in this book, the contact with your home is pretty steady and doesn't require letters very often. Or all the exercises may spur your letter-writing habit even more!

# Passion

## Stayin' alive

Just as with any organism/structure that holds life, there has to be some system in place that assures your home will maintain its vitality. Certainly general upkeep and care counts for something and should not be minimized, but in addition there should be a level of care that extends past the basics of keeping the floors swept and the windows clean. You might call this nurturing the grace of the home—those actions that not only keep the place alive but also instill a sense of uniqueness and of beauty. However, it's not just a decorative approach that is important for vitality, but also a connection with the changes of nature. A home's life should be coupled with appropriate timing, so that the grace or vitality is not just a design element but a timely design element. Just like some people wear green on St. Patrick's Day or put on costumes at Halloween, your house can also take on this visual marker of temporal change. A perfect example of this is holiday decorations.

Each year during the holidays, a home will be enhanced with nonessential yet beautiful and hopefully meaningful symbols that can represent the owner's religion, culture, and memories. Many times these symbolic actions extend to the outside of the home as well. After the holidays, the symbolic decorations are removed. The importance of this action is that the house was included in an event that is dependent on timing.

Some of my clients have shown me other ways to include the home in this temporal dimension—ways that indicate where we are in the cycle of life by looking at our home. One client has her summer furniture arrangement and her winter furniture arrangement. Some of this is driven by how the sun

enters her space so she maximizes this feature by the placement of her sofa and chairs. In addition, she has a summer rug
and a winter rug that she changes accordingly. She replaces
pillows on the sofa to reflect the seasonal change and to match
the corresponding rug. This process only takes one Saturday
morning and she does it by herself. In the end, her home
reflects her intention of wholeness and peace filtered through
the appropriate season.

Another client collected twelve silk wreaths over the years.
On the first of each month, she places a new wreath on her
front door to mark the change of time. Some of the wreaths
she made herself, others were gifts. Each one has a story and
a meaning which she remembers and savors as she puts up a
new wreath. She has found an ingenious way to store them
so that they're easily accessible and are protected as they
wait for their particular month to cycle around. When she
drives up to her home, she need only look at her front door
to be reminded what month it is. I've had another client who
accomplished a similar idea with wreaths which she changed
four times a year based on the season.

A well-traveled and cosmopolitan couple I worked with
came up with a way to take this idea of bringing time into their
home through the use of artwork. On each solstice or equinox,
they celebrate an "artwork exchange" evening when they take
down a painting over the fireplace and replace it with another.
The paintings were found on one of their art buying trips to
the southwest and are all by the same artist. They follow the
seasons—summer, winter, fall, and spring. They're similar
in size, similar in style, yet depict a different timeframe. This
little ritual often includes a glass of wine, some music, maybe a

friend or two. Their home has an internal clock keeping itself and the occupants in step with nature.

The idea of a summer bedroom and a winter bedroom is not a new one. The change of seasons is marked by different comforters, different curtains, and a rug change, to name a few ideas. Since we don't live our lives without taking into account the season or the month, our homes should also be keeping track of this dimension. As people, we change our wardrobe depending on the season. We wear one kind of clothing when the temperatures are hot and humid, and another kind when the temperatures drop below zero. Why wouldn't we "outfit" our home to reflect what season it is, or month, or even day?

Unfortunately our spaces have been created to reflect generic seasons—all the same. Although a home may be beautiful, decluttered, and stylish, if it looks the same day in and day out, month after month, it's flat. The windows may be opened more regularly in warm weather while the screened porch may closed up during the cold months, but other than that no other indication tells us we've moved from one season to another.

Another argument for changing the space in accordance with time is that the occupants embrace the time change in a whole different way. Keeping track of days and months on a calendar is a linear way of passing time; feeling the change in your home by looking at it is a visceral way of integrating time. We have taken the cycle of nature and moved it into our home. We may not have spring buds coming up through the carpet, but we have a fresh arrangement of furniture or a piece of artwork to remind us of where we are on the continuum. We certainly understand the three-dimensionality of our homes when we consider the relationship of furniture, the perspective down a hall, or the impact of a mirror. Yet the fourth dimension of time is rarely incorporated.

Aside from integrating the time element, changing the space on a regular basis, even in small ways, keeps your interest peaked. Even though you yourself may have changed the pillows to the summer ones earlier in the day, it takes several days before their surprise diminishes. Coming around the corner or first entering the room, there's an endearing reminder of change, of a new phase. You don't lose interest in your home because it continues to amaze you on a regular basis. When your house is keeping time, so are you. You're both staying alive.

Due to a family emergency out of town, I had to stay over night in a motel near the hospital. I reserved a room over the phone, sight unseen. When I got to the motel at the end of a difficult day, I was hoping to unwind, relax, and get my thoughts together. Instead I drove up to a rundown, poorly lit place on a dark side street. The room was obviously a smoking one. The bedspread had seen better days, and although clean, the bathroom was in shabby condition. After a long and emotional day, I was exhausted. There was no phone in the room and I just didn't have the strength to go back to the front desk and ask for another room, let alone start looking for another motel at that hour of the night. I resigned myself to making the best of it.

I opened the window to let in fresh air and get the energy flowing again. I hung my car keys on the doorknob as a protective measure—I would hear the keys rattle if someone tried to break in. I removed the bedspread, folded back the top sheet and blanket, fluffed the pillows, and found a piece of gum in my purse to put on my pillow (a chocolate piece would have been great but didn't have any on me). I unpacked my pajamas and spread them on the bed, and carefully hung up my clothes.

The bathtub looked usable so I filled it up with hot water, turned off the lights except for one small one in the bedroom, and soaked the day away. After thirty minutes when I came back into the bedroom, I was astounded at how the room had taken on new energy. It looked inviting, charming, and safe. I crawled into bed and slept undisturbed until 9:30 AM. I woke up to my cell phone ringing—my family was wondering where I was.

That was a good lesson in transforming space in small ways to make a huge difference. After the motel experience, I went home and decided to see if that same transformation could happen in other spaces. I had the same kind of transformative experience happen again and again—from a fruit cellar to my office closet, a basement storage area to a corner of the garage. With small considerations and mostly small financial investment, each space transformed to become something more than it had been.

Keeping your space alive may mean addressing and transforming those dead spaces in your home. They may be corners you have forgotten about or would like to forget about. They may have become a catch-all.

The following exercise will help you see for yourself the magic and charm that can happen in the most obscure places.

**Finding sacred in the shadows**

1. Find the shadow place
Walk around your house and find a place that is neglected or ignored. This may be a storage closet, furnace room, pantry, or attic. It will probably be a place you go to only when you have to; otherwise, it remains a corner/room/area that seldom sees the light of day.

2. Make it functional
Start by straightening out the items and cleaning the area. This will probably be the most challenging step. Get rid of things that need to be removed. Fix anything that's broken. You might simply haul out everything that is in the space and then one-by-one decide what goes back and what doesn't.

3. Beautify
Once the physical objects have found some kind of order, find a way to make it better, by bringing in a touch of beauty or a small way to class it up. Some ideas are: a new doorknob, better lighting or a brighter bulb, a rug, silk flowers, windchime, cheerful poster, etc. None of these suggestions needs to be costly, yet any one of them can still shift the experience of being there.

4. Love it
Appreciate what you did to enliven a part of your home. If you didn't often go to that spot, make a point to do so now. You will see how the feelings of dread have turned to anticipation and pride when you see how the place has transformed.

> Every place—the concert hall, classroom, factory,
> and marketplace—can be sacred if the murmuring
> of the soul is allowed to shape the walls.
> —*The Temples in the House,* Anthony Lawlor

We have a small cellar room under our front entry. It's cold and, well, creepy. For several years we discussed what to do with it as it became the catch-all for stuff. It's not heated, very damp and very small. One day we decided on a plan and took action. We removed everything from the room, scrubbed the walls and the floor, painted them with a cement block sealer, put in rust-proof shelving and a new light bulb. We put back only the items we were going to use and set them purposefully on the shelves. I love just looking in there—not to mention I can always find the can of paint for the living room if I need it, or touchup varnish for a piece of furniture. It's right there on those shelves, labeled, accessible.

Even a space that is hardly ever seen warrants this attention. Even the gloomiest spots can become special. No space is hopeless; rather it waits for your caring hand to bring it to life.

## An ailing house

The premise under which Georgine called me was that she had been sick and troubled ever since she and her husband moved into their new home three years prior. Her illnesses included two bouts with pneumonia, shingles, a persistent cough, and her husband was now diagnosed with a benign growth on one of his lungs. Chinese medicine describes lung and skin issues as a sign of grief so I came armed with appropriate questions about their grief issues. But they didn't have any grief issues. In fact, they were happy to be in the house, designed it themselves, and loved everything about it. They just had been dealing with uncharacteristic health issues.

When I asked about the building process and the history of the land, Georgine gave me a clue about what might be the cause of their distress. It seems the entire development had been owned by a farmer, who was the fifth generation in his family to be working that land. Economic hard times forced the man to sell his land to a developer.

The relationship between the developer and the farmer turned into a bitter one. The farmer accused the developer of not paying him the agreed-upon amount of money; the developer contended he was following their agreement, meanwhile putting up 50 houses as part of his initial phase of development. The farmer lived in the original farm house at the end of the road—a stark contrast to the enormous homes being built right in front of him.

Georgine said on several occasions during the building process they would drive out to their site to see how the construction was going only to see that somehow the farmer had managed to stop any further development from happening. A lot of vandalism occurred. The developer accused the farmer of creating the vandalism and of impeding progress; the farmer, in his 80s, said he couldn't have caused such damage because of his age and frailty. The developer tried to put a restraining order on the farmer. Georgine shared that each week there was a catastrophe or a drama. Their home and the homes of all the other buyers were caught in the middle. Needless to say they were very happy to finally be in their dream home. The developer had moved onto the second phase of building; the farmer had retreated to his home, defeated and ailing.

Now that they were finally settled in their home, it was disappointing they were both dealing with all these health issues. They had moved in healthy and now one or the other was always having some kind of medical emergency. They were even beginning to wonder if they actually liked the house at all, since it seemed ever since they had moved in they were sick.

Based on the connection between the home and its occupants, it seemed clear to me their issues were stemming directly from the origins of the house. The house was erected with feelings of anger, betrayal, mistrust, and a sense of loss. Whether the seller of the land was accurate about the behavior of the buyer, he was putting forth enormous grief and regret. These feelings were picked up by the most vulnerable feature—the half-built homes. It wasn't surprising when I learned that everyone in the development, without exception, was sick; a couple of people had actually died. Several of the homes were for sale—people desperately trying to escape what was going on there.

A home can most definitely be ailing. The causes can be from a turbulent and messy building process, as in Georgine's case, or it can be from the people who live there who are themselves ailing in some way. A house won't necessarily get sick just because someone living there has allergies or was recently diagnosed with diabetes. In fact, that might be when a home will step forward to help. A house's ailments come about when laws are being broken—like drug-dealing, prostitution, harboring stolen goods, abuse. A home can get sick when someone, for whatever reason, no longer takes care of it.

Typically it's easy to see when a home is ailing because it falls into disrepair. The initial symptoms may not be obvious to someone driving by (like a furnace that should be fixed and is ignored, or a roof that leaked into a bedroom, or a sliding closet door that falls off the track). Eventually, however, the symptoms of the illness move outside. Luckily there are a lot of people who look specifically for these homes—fixer-uppers. Their mission is to take them, fix them up, and heal them of their pain.

Recently a news broadcast told of a crack house operating three blocks from us. I knew instantly where that house was located because I'd drive by that home nearly every day and wonder what was going on behind those drapes. The paint was peeling, the lawn had dried up over the summer, the curtains were always drawn, and one of the windows was cracked. It was obvious to see that it was ill compared to the neighboring homes.

Georgine's house didn't fit this category. It was sick but thus far maintained its new and fresh look. It wouldn't take long, however, before there would be some telltale signs that something wasn't right. The abundance of For Sale signs scattered throughout the development was one telling piece of evidence. Eventually, whether through dead landscaping or peeling paint, something else would indicate that all was not whole and balanced in those homes.

Obviously, cleaning and fixing up a home that desperately needs it will shift its condition to a healthier one. However, whether there are physical features that need to be repaired or not, an ailing home needs assistance in getting to a healthier place. One way is to make a direct and deliberate contact with your home by writing a reassuring letter, outlining what your plans are to make it better. Writing a thank you to your home can go a long way in bringing some relief to a troubled and ailing space. Appreciation is always a good approach to healing a troubled situation.

Writing a thank you note to your home is particularly helpful when you're unhappy with your home for whatever reason. Maybe it has needed repairs, maintenance, or just hasn't been fulfilling. Rather than looking to move or harboring resentments, a cheaper and easier action to take is to write your home a thank you note. This is also a great exercise if you have positive feelings about your home and simply want to acknowledge what it is doing for you.

If you have any anger or resentments toward your house, you may want to go for a walk to change your state of mind before taking pen to paper. You may even want to do this exercise away from your home, in a neutral place, like a coffee shop or a library where you will be relatively certain you'll be undisturbed.

If you aren't having any particular issues with your home and, in fact, have been able to find a nice connection with it, this exercise will be very easy for you to do and very enjoyable.

## Writing a thank you to your home

1. Special note paper
To make this exercise more special, use an actual thank you note or special stationery. Because they are typically not very big in size you will be forced to be succinct and direct.

2. Salutation
Start with the name of your home, if you have one:

Dear . . . , or Dear Home, is fine as well.

3. Reasons for writing

List two reasons you are thankful for your home. Some examples might be:

> I want to thank you for keeping us warm through this long, hard winter.

> Thank you for being a steady beacon for us while we've been gone so much.

> Thank you for making me feel safe.

> I appreciate your patience when I don't have time to clean very often.

> I appreciate how beautiful you are. You make me very proud.

Feel free to think of your own special reasons why you're thankful. If you can think of no reason to thank your space, make up something. Just as in difficult relationships with people, there is always some aspect for which you can find gratitude for your house, even if it's simply for having the experience of living there.

4. Pay back

End with one intention that you commit to doing concerning the house:

> It is my intention to get the bathroom painted this spring.

> I will fix the electrical issue in the bedroom next month.

> It is my plan to do something about the back door before winter.

If you don't have a specific project in mind or you feel like you have completed most everything that needs to be done, then you can promise that you'll continue with needed maintenance, or you can commit to a long life together.

5. Keep in a special place
Place the thank-you note in a special place in your home. This might be in the drawer of your nightstand, or under a plant in the kitchen, or if you have a scrapbook for your home, paste it in there.

## Making the house something it isn't

Terry bought her duplex after a divorce in the hopes that the money from the rental unit would pay her mortgage. That did indeed happen, giving her a chance to rebuild the losses she incurred from a bitter and difficult marriage. Nevertheless, as the years went by, she would intermittently wake up in the middle of the night convinced that she had heard someone walking through her space, but no one was there. In one instance, she was so certain there was an intruder she quietly dialed the police in the dark only to realize that, again, no one was actually there. She had ghost busters come through but none of them picked up on any wandering spirits.

When I began working with her, she repeated the story she had told others over and over again. Something or someone kept waking her up in the night. She admitted she had never heard unusual noises, just sensed a presence. I was inspired to tell her to take note of her dreams in the upcoming weeks and see if there might be a connection. Meanwhile, I recommended she sleep in another bedroom—a better location in terms of the front door and because it might just stop her sleepless nights.

A couple weeks later she called me to say she had been awakened again. But before she got herself involved in the drama, she spent a moment recalling what she had been dreaming just before her "wake-up call." She shared that in her dream she had been eating donut holes—piles of them. Terry wasn't one to eat sugar so she couldn't figure out what it might mean. Knowing that dreams are never literal, we were exploring other possible meanings around the symbol of donut holes, being hole, hole-ness. I asked whether her house had been built as a duplex or made into a duplex later. When I was there, I could see that possibly the house had been built as a one-family house. As with many older homes, someone often converts them to multiple housing units. Terry had assumed it had been built as a duplex, but would try to find out.

Within a few hours, Terry called back and confirmed that the house had been built as a single-family home. Then in the 1950s had been converted to a duplex. Is it possible the home wanted to be whole? she wondered, and the donut holes were symbolic of that message?

I told her about writing to her home to actively put her in contact with the space so she could validate the assumption that her house was trying to get her attention at night. She told me she would do that but assured me that she already knew the answer—yes, the house wanted to be whole. Although it had not occurred to her before, she LOVED the idea.

Terry did write several letters to her house, some of which were thank you notes. Meanwhile she considered her options with regard to turning it back into a single family home. A few months later, opportunities came her way. Just as an unexpected inheritance arrived, her tenants informed her of their job transfer. Terry was able to move forward, converting her duplex into a single home, in line with its original configuration. She continues to live in her "whole" house and continues to sleep peacefully through the night.

A conversion of a single family home into two units needs to happen with a great deal of sensitivity. The house was not built that way and will generally rebel in some fashion. This is even more of an issue when doors are locked between the two, requiring separate entrances. As Terry's story elaborates, some kind of disturbance could occur. There might be health issues or wealth challenges when the house is split in two. The energy shift is enormous and can only be successfully carried out when there has been some kind of blessing done to the home—even after the fact, a blessing will help.

The few times I've seen this change actually work was when a lower level/basement area was converted into a mother-in-law apartment. This was successful because the only change that was needed was the addition of a small kitchenette and because the doors between the two levels were never locked—closed, maybe, for privacy, but never locked—the energy could continue to move between the two places. Furthermore, there was still only one front door that both parties used.

There is a corresponding challenge when the change occurs in reverse: two condo units are made into one big one, or a duplex built with side-by-side units is converted into one space. Dividing walls have to be removed and a kitchen has to be dismantled. The kitchen corresponds to the health of the occupants as well as the harmony between them. Having more than one kitchen in a space can represent a challenge with health and/or separation between family members. One of the front doors has to be physically eliminated or certainly downplayed so there's no confusion about how to get into this new space, and therefore no corresponding confusion in the occupants' lives. By changing the original structural intention of the space, its integrity has been compromised. Short of converting it back to what it was intended, some critical actions should occur to bring it to a new sense of balance and harmony. This can be done through a ritual or blessing.

Of course, this leads to the question of converting an old building into high-end condos. Originally the building was a factory; suddenly it becomes a series of homes. The difference in this case is that the building has usually fallen into disrepair. It may even have been saved from being destroyed by a far-sighted developer. In this case, it is better to have the building renovated for a different use than be demolished. I generally see this situation bring about positive outcomes for the people who live there. It's as though the building has been given a second chance and expresses gratitude through its support to the current occupants.

On a smaller scale, it is common for me to suggest to a client that they convert an empty bedroom into an office, or to change their dining room, which is never used, to a library which would be used. Typically these kinds of changes take place without a hitch; I hear the client say how much they appreciate using their space in a new way. Using a room is better than not using it at all.

One of my clients converted an awkwardly placed dining room that was right near the front entry. From a practical standpoint it was on the other end of the house from the kitchen making it difficult to use—and he never did. I suggested he change it into a parlor, an inviting and comfortable place to welcome guests. He loved it so much, most evenings he gravitates to this new room to read or listen to music.

Yet, there is a limit where a change like this becomes too dramatic and where it abandons the integrity of the original intention of the house. For instance, trying to change a garage into something other than a garage can bring insurmountable issues. Garages hold a different kind of energy—one that does not support long-term habitation. It might work as an office where someone working there keeps their focus and their attention charged up. But, that said, I've seen where all that charged energy still doesn't offset the fact that cars used to drive into the space. In a short while, the person sitting in the garage/office becomes overwhelmed and, well, "exhaust"-ed. Even trying to turn a garage into a family room didn't work out for some of my clients, who got divorced shortly after they completed the conversion.

Another change that occurs that has serious structural as well as energetic implications is when the front door is moved or removed. People do this for a number of reasons not realizing what kind of turmoil they may be unleashing. In Feng Shui, the front door is defined as the metaphorical point at which opportunities enter and where good luck arrives. No one should confuse this path. Any positive aspects will be diffused and weakened if they have to travel to a side door or a back door, or look for a new front door located around the corner.

The rationale that the occupants never use the front door is not a valid reason to get rid of it. An entry pattern was established when the home or building was first built; it may have been in place for years. That pattern should not be broken or altered—ever. The front door is such a pivotal feature of a home that the fallout from moving it can range from health issues, losing jobs, having car accidents, marriage issues, to all of these at once.

When a client moves into a space that has been significantly altered or alters it themselves without understanding the ramifications, I suggest they help the space "heal." Just as anyone would comfort and support a child who had undergone serious surgery, an occupant needs to comfort and support their space. This is done by care, maintenance, update, upkeep, blessings. Fix what needs to be fixed; clean what needs to be cleaned; paint, polish, and perfect all parts of the space to the best of their ability and resources. Over time they may find their space has adjusted to the new configuration or they may be drawn to return the space back to what it was originally intended to be.

To underscore the idea and the importance of understanding the original intention of your home, it can be helpful to take photos of it—from different angles, close-up, far away. It gives you a literal and figurative snapshot of what your home looks like. Sometimes, we just don't see its features for what they truly are; sometimes we just don't appreciate the home that we have.

Before a recent block party in our neighborhood, an insightful and ambitious realtor went up and down the street and took pictures of each of our homes. During the course of the evening, we each wore the photo of our home on name tags she had created for each person. Although we may have walked or driven by a particular house for years, we had never known the people who lived there. The vacant house on the corner was suddenly filled with trikes in the yard and lights on at night, but we didn't know the people. Now, because of this simple name tag, we could connect the house with the owners in a fun and relaxed way. It made a visceral connection between people and structure, inhabitants and place.

The next sunny day I went out and took pictures of our house. It was fall and leaves were all over the ground, covering the sidewalk. I printed out all the photos, selected my favorite, and put it in a little frame on my desk. The irony of having a picture of the outside of the house sitting in the inside of the house did cross my mind. I appreciated being able to look at it because I saw the house in a more objective way. The camera creates a distance or objectivity that eludes the eye. Eventually I took a picture in the middle of winter, in the spring and in the summer to round out all four seasons. I change the photographs as the seasons change.

## Photographing your home

Here are some suggestions if you want to objectively see where you live and, in turn, maximize your connection with the place you call home.

### 1. Take various photos

Take your camera and stand about 20–30 feet from the front of your home and take as many photos of your house as you feel necessary. Gradually, walk toward your house taking more pictures as you go. Eventually, you will be about 5–6 feet in front of your front door.

## 2. Pick your favorite
Look over all the photographs and decide which one best represents your home. It may be a close-up of the front door or it may be one that includes the door and part of the house or it may be the entire place. Select the one that says "home" to you.

## 3. Place of honor
Put it in a frame or stand it up somewhere obvious. Place it where it won't get buried or overlooked. From time to time you may find yourself looking at the photo. Eventually you may find yourself more actively connecting by talking to the photo or asking questions of it.

## 4. Keep photo current
When some time has passed, perhaps another season, go back outside to the exact spot of the first photo and take another one. Replace the first photo with the new one or get another frame so both can be displayed. See how it feels to now relate to your home under different circumstances.

## 5. One for each season
Repeat Step #4, no less than a total of four times.

It's important to keep the same angle and distance on your favorite photos so that you aren't distracted by different information. This doesn't mean you can't change things like painting the house a different color, or hanging a different wreath on your front door, or removing a diseased tree. What you're tracking is the cycle of time as it affects your home. You're becoming a witness to the life that it is expressing.

If you decide to simultaneously display many versions of your home taken at different times of the year, I urge you to be careful so that this project doesn't turn into a form of clutter. Much like people who want to put up photos of their kids through all stages of their lives, you will want to selectively show representations, not every single step.

Photographing your home on a regular basis will help you "see" it again and, in turn, maximize your connection with the place you call home. You will look at your place with a new perspective and will be aware when anything starts to change. By taking pictures of your house, you're not only tracking the cycle of time as it affects your space, but you're also becoming a witness to the life that it expresses in such subtle and charming ways that you would not capture by simply looking at it with your own eyes. Within the framework of a photo, details become important and obvious and you'll notice when anything starts to change.

As these images find a place in your home, they will also find a place in your heart and you will look at them as if you were looking at a dear friend—which is what this is all about.

## PROTECTION

### Death at the door

Melanie, a friend of a client, had been suddenly diagnosed with a fast-moving cancer. Her medical team was surprised she had not experienced symptoms long before her diagnosis since her disease was so extensive. At this point, there was no surgery that could save her. They predicted she would have about four months to live, the last two of which would be in a nursing home under round-the-clock care.

She went home to begin the last days of her life. Her children started the process of checking into nursing homes, assuring Melanie they would only place her in the best location. Melanie, however, argued that she would never go to a nursing home, ever. She would die at home no matter what it would take.

Her children assumed she was not thinking clearly and quietly proceeded with plans for her last days. All three adult children knew themselves well enough to know that none of them would be in a position to care for her themselves in order to honor her request to stay at home.

As the weeks went by, Melanie's strength failed. She was eating less and sleeping more, yet she was still waking up to her familiar room with its familiar sounds. Her children took turns being with her at all times, but they knew it would soon be time to get her into a facility. They didn't discuss it with their mother for fear of upsetting her but hoped that when the time came, she would not register clearly what was happening and would let them transport her out of her home.

On one particular day, all three of Melanie's children had to be away from her for a short period of time. She was barely managing on her own at this point, so her oldest daughter made sure she was comfortable in her bed before she left. A younger daughter would be arriving 20 minutes later. Melanie smiled and assured her she was fine, she'd take a nap, and looked forward to seeing her again soon.

The younger daughter arrived to find that despite her mother's strong vital signs earlier that day, Melanie had died in those few moments she was left alone. No one could deny she looked peaceful and satisfied. She had died at home, just as she had wished. Nevertheless, all of her children bemoaned the fact they had left her alone. They second-guessed that if someone had been there with her she may still be alive.

I presume that may be true. However, for a brief moment, Melanie found herself surrounded by a love that could let her go. Just as her house had watched her adult life unfold, it was appropriate the house help her move onto her next home—no strings, no regrets, just unconditional love and support. She was free to leave. Even though it may have been earlier than predicted, she took her exit when she could and while she was still in her home.

Most people who are consciously dying want to be able to die at home. Although family and friends will try to accommodate that request, they often feel it's in the best interest of the patient to get them to a facility where they'll have adequate care. Regardless of quality of care, I've found that people would still rather be home, where they can recognize their surroundings. Typically, but not always, home is quieter. Usually the food is homemade. In quiet moments, a dying person wants to open their eyes and be able to trust their surroundings. There's safety in this familiarity.

The house, too, wants this experience. Over the years it may have been witness to parties, reunions, babies, kids growing up, birthdays, middle-of-the-night anguish, arguments, and reconciliations. The house can offer immense support during this final transition. When someone dies at home, they are surrounded by a sanctuary that may have been doing its safe-keeping job for years for the individual—someone who knows their dreams and is willing to help them with their next step.

Some homes just understand how to transition people in

a peaceful and graceful way. I personally know two people who died at home alone unexpectedly. They were found later, one in her bedroom, one in her living room. Both were going about the daily routine of their lives when the moment came. Although we were all saddened, I heard many people say "At least she was home." It didn't change the outcome, but it said a lot about the process. In other words, they were both safe when they died. I argue that perhaps they weren't alone after all, but instead were guided and embraced during their transition. That may be what we all want at the moment of death— an embrace of reassurance. Both of these women had lived in their homes over 40 years. It stands to reason they would have a guardian until the end of their time.

Nevertheless, there are times when concerned family members or friends are forced to make the difficult decision of taking an elderly or dying person out of their home and for good reason. The patient's safety is at risk and their ability to take care of themselves is diminishing. Despite these good intentions, there are countless stories about the vulnerable person making a rapid decline in their health and dying shortly after settling in to a strange place. Having left their home, they've left behind what they've come to know and love—the familiar sights, sounds they recognize, smells they know all too well—a dear friend. Now they must adjust to new faces, a new kind of food, and a different room. Too many changes.

Sometimes a person has no choice in the matter as to whether to stay at home or to go elsewhere for care. Well-meaning family may decide what's best for them, or the urgency of their needs has escalated urgently requiring a physical move. The patient may not have had time to say goodbye to their home. They long for their home, just as their home may be longing for them. Something unfinished lingers between the two of them. Loneliness can break the strongest of spirits.

This doesn't mean families must take on the responsibility of caring for their loved ones at all costs. I know all too well that many of us are not cut out to be a caregiver. It does mean, however, that there must be a moment to bring closure to a bond that may have lasted over many years. Both sides of this relationship (the person and the house) need to acknowledge the separation, whatever that might mean and whatever form that might take. It may be as simple as a few quiet moments of gratitude. It may be a letter that's written. It may even mean someone else has to do it for them if the person leaving can no longer do it for themselves. The connection between a person and their home deserves the dignity of a goodbye.

## Does a house die?

Roger and Marlys bought a beautiful home out in the country where they could grow vegetables, raise horses and be away from the noises inherent to a city. Along with their property they also inherited a tiny ramshackle cottage that sat off to the side, but visible from their driveway. They were uncertain of what it was ever used for so initially they planned to tear it down. Before the demolition had been scheduled, Marlys walked over to the dilapidated and sad little place to look inside. She saw that it had once been a working cottage—a makeshift kitchen had been installed as well as plumbing for a bathroom.

Marlys sat on a window ledge and took in the energy of the place. It had a great view out the back of what was going to be their vegetable garden. On the other side, it looked into a grove of trees. It was essentially two rooms with a bathroom—big enough for a guest or two, or appropriate as a studio for herself. Roger couldn't believe it when she told him at dinner that night that she wanted to keep the cottage and renovate it.

It was as though the cottage spoke to her—that's how she described her decision. Although it looked like a pathetic heap of wood and broken glass, inside there was a spark that was alive and willing to burn bright again. Roger agreed to her idea but only on the condition that they spend no money on labor—Marlys herself was going to have to fix it up. She was undaunted by this offer.

Over the next two years, little by little she found ways to transform a sad place into a charming one. She figured out how to fix the floor and put in new windows. She managed to repair the door on the front, and with the help of Roger, they installed some recycled cabinets. All along she wasn't sure what the end product was going to be used for. She only knew she had to save the life of this cottage.

Now that the cottage has been insulated and rewired (by Roger), Marlys uses it primarily as a writing study. When Roger is at work during the day, she fixes her lunch out there, looks out the windows, and lets the inspiration come. She does have a foldout sofa which suffices when her sister visits. Everyone who comes to their home comments on the cottage off in the distance because its appeal and magnetism is hypnotic. Marlys truly did save the space and infuse life back into it.

It's rare that a house "dies." It may certainly encounter disaster, but often there's a possibility of rebuilding the same place or salvaging what is left. Even if there's been a fire or a tornado, there generally are enough remnants to recapture the original home. Typically the lifespan of a house or building can be hundreds of years, if we let it. However, homes or buildings are torn down because it may be cheaper to start over, or the owner doesn't want to bother with the old structure, enamored with the idea of something new, or someone is tired of the old place.

I find it difficult to watch television coverage of a building being planted with dynamite in order to bring it down at a precise moment in a precise manner. For years the structure served an important function only to be reduced to a pile of rubble. In the interest of progress, there were probably no arrangements for a memorial or plans to rescue any unique or special features to be reused in a new building.

One night on a home makeover show, I watched the contractor take the trailer that had once been a family home to a big-wheel competition where it was destroyed. Granted, it had been undersized for the family and had a roof leak and didn't look the best, but I watched in disbelief as the family cheered while their home was demolished by trucks with gargantuan wheels. What was once the little girl's bedroom was ripped apart while she cheered them on. The possibility of fixing up the trailer and giving it to someone else to use wasn't considered. Maybe it was beyond saving, but the lack of respect shown a place that one day was their home, no matter the condition, and the next day the source of ridicule, was heartbreaking.

For whatever reason, a home or building can certainly get to the point of no-return, where it actually becomes cheaper to tear it down and start over. It's hard to fault someone for making that decision. Yet, without thought to the idea that the house held memories, fulfilled its responsibilities, provided protection, and contained conscious essence and breath, a home is demolished, whether by big wheel trucks or a demolition ball.

From an ecological point of view, salvaging a home is a better choice. Although it may seem as though the space is dead and unresponsive, its life is dormant and can be revived. Often these second versions are better than the original one, as the house is being upgraded, improved, and enhanced. Typically this kind of commitment comes from someone who truly appreciates the place and its uniqueness and therefore works with heartfelt concern and respect. Who wouldn't flourish under that kind of attention?

That said, homes are torn down every day without giving it a second thought. I've had clients who've scheduled the demolition crew to take out an old house, with the plans for a new, bigger home to take its place. Sometimes the old structure is already gone when I get there. They all want me to help them site their new place. It's hard for me to get past the sadness and feeling of loss as I stand on the land trying to imagine the new improved version. If possible, I have the clients take something from the old structure that they can use in the new one—a drawer pull, a window casing, wood planks that can be part of the floor. One client took the ornate furnace grate from the place they were tearing down and used it as a partition in their new home. It acts as a memorial to a place that once held a family's life, was witness to holiday celebrations, protected and warmed as needed, and that truly was alive.

I personally witnessed a thoughtful honoring of the death and rebirth of a space was when I was working with a couple who inherited a family home. It was located in a small town where the husband's father had lived all his life. They took many weekend trips to assess the property and to try to come to some conclusion about the direction they were going to take. Not only did his father live his entire life in the house, but Jeff did as well, so the memories stacked up through a couple of generations. Most of the memories came not from the house itself but from a garage/workshop/shed that was in the back of the house. By the time Jeff and his wife had inherited the house, the shed had collapsed. It truly looked "dead."

Yet, each time they visited, Jeff would rummage through the rubble and come up with a long-forgotten memory of something his dad taught him or told him. It was where he first learned to change oil in the car; it was where his dad taught him to cut mitred corners; it was where he parked his first car; it was where he had his first kiss. Jeff couldn't let the shed just lie there and he couldn't haul the stuff away, so he decided to rebuild it.

Little by little, during their weekend trips and vacations during the summer, he put his shed back together. He interspersed new materials along with the old ones. He used whatever he could and created a workshop for himself. In his words, the shed "had a rebirth." It gave him ideas about where to relocate the big window so he could maximize the sunlight. It nudged him to put in more electrical outlets than he thought he'd ever need, but when it was finished he needed every one of them. The space suggested an overhead fan to keep the air circulating and relocation of an infrared heater, both of which ended up being perfectly situated.

The workshop stands as a tribute to a man who listened to his space. Jeff has started a parttime woodworking business in his shed. A sign to that effect has appeared on the front. He looks forward to his retirement when he can spend most of his time within a space that embraces him, supports him, and was built with his own dreams in mind. How can he not succeed under these circumstances?

## A letter from your house

Communicating with your home is a subtle and delicate assignment. It's easy to miss the message or discover the dialogue. An exercise that can help nail down a more concrete form of conversation is to open yourself up to getting a letter from your home.

If you've gotten a special journal in which to write your letters and thank-you notes to your home, then this is the perfect place in which to put the responses. If not, paper and pen will work as well. Writing in your home's scrapbook is also an appropriate option.

### 1. Quiet time

Plan some quiet time when you will not be disturbed. This exercise requires an inner connection that needs your focused attention.

### 2. Address the house

Say or think the name of your house three times. If you haven't named it, you can use your address or simply use the word Home or House.

### 3. Connect

Sit for a few minutes resting in the assurance that you have connected with the spirit of your home. Pay attention to what that connection feels like and name it: sweet, loving, protective, tentative, shy, etc.

### 4. Salutation to yourself

Take your journal or paper and write Dear (your name) at the top. Some people, when doing exercises like this, feel they can get out of their own way by writing with their non-dominant hand. If this feels appropriate, I encourage you to try it. Otherwise, whatever hand you normally write with is fine.

### 5. Become the house

Write the words: What I love about you is . . .
and complete the sentence, remembering that the "I" in that sentence is the house, and the "you" is you—the house is going to tell you something it loves about you. If you think you can't make the connection, then pretend you're tuned into the house. From this posture of "pretend," what do you think your house would say to you?

### 6. Pretend the answers

Then write the words: My favorite time with you is . . .
Complete this sentence as though your house is telling you when it really enjoys being with you. If you think you aren't connecting, pretend that you are.

### 7. Listen to what your house is saying

Write: I regret that . . .
Again, the house is telling you what it regrets.

### 8. Let it thank you

Write the words: Thank you for . . .
Listen to what your home thanks you for. You may be surprised and thrilled at the answer.

### 9. Love & kisses

Finally, let the house sign off with an ending. It may just end with "Sincerely" or "Thanks again" or it may have one last thought to add. Don't be in a hurry to end the letter in case there's a last word or two from your home. Be patient and allow the house plenty of time to react. If this is the first time you've communicated with your home, the connection may be weak and tenuous.

### 10. Signature

At this time, if your home has a name, that would be an appropriate way to close the letter. If it doesn't have a name, this might be an opportunity for the house to tell you what its name is. If you don't get a name, don't work too hard at this. A name will come eventually—one that you know is right.

### 11. Keep in a special place

Place this letter in your house scrapbook or somewhere special where you could reread at a later date. Let whatever information or feelings you got when you were receiving the letter settle into your heart. I wouldn't suggest you respond right away, but instead take some time to integrate and reflect.

# Parting

## Losing your home

Unfortunately, there are times when people lose their homes—due to fire, earthquake, explosion, tornado, flood, divorce or foreclosure. The house simply no longer exists in their lives. Parts of it may be scattered around due to high winds or parts of it may be buried under rubble because of an explosion or earthquake. It may be permanently chained closed until its financial issues can be unraveled, or someone else may have taken ownership and you no longer have a key. However it happens, there may come a time when a space is dead to you.

It isn't until your home is gone that you realize how strongly your life is structured around having a place to land at the end of the day and a place to wake up to in the morning. It isn't just the inconvenience of not having a roof over your head, there's a psychological loss that is far greater than the physical items. Using the Feng Shui metaphor that your space reflects your life, it would follow that if your space is gone, your life could likewise seem to disappear. Not only have you lost memories and mementos, but also the possibility of future memories that could have been created in the home.

If, by some unfortunate circumstance, your home is "gone," acknowledge the situation and find a way to grieve. Whether you've had to move to someone else's house, a hotel, a temporary apartment, or a homeless shelter, take a moment to remember your home.

## Memorial to your home

### 1. Memory corner
Determine where you can set up a "memorial" to your home—a shelf, a dresser, your desk. You may want to place a scarf or a piece of lace on the surface to delineate it as a special spot.

### 2. Memento
Choose a memento or a picture of the home that is now lost to you. If your home was destroyed by natural causes, you

may be able to find something on the site that has meaning for you—part of a light fixture, a handle from a kitchen drawer, a door knob. If there are no remains or you can't secure any, then draw a picture of your home or a part of your home that you loved.

### 3. Plant or flowers
Place the memento or drawing on the fabric along with something that represents life and growth—a plant or flowers. You may use silk if that is better suited to your lifestyle.

### 4. Show up
Spend a little time each day in front of this shrine to the home that you lost. This is the time to grieve or to be angry or to express regrets. Speak to the home and tell it how you feel. Although the physical house may be gone, its spirit is still close by and would appreciate a word or two from you. Include the home as part of your process until you no longer need it.

### Movin' on
Since a space has only your best interests at heart, it follows that when it's time for you to leave, it will let you know. Of course, whether we can discern its subtle message is another matter. You may have been arguing with yourself for some time about moving, vacillating between it being a good idea and a really bad one. There may have been moments when you daydreamed about living in another place, even a different geographical area, but then dismissed it as unrealistic, improbable, or impossible.

Yet those ideas come from somewhere. If they don't serve to recommit you to the space you're in, then perhaps their message is worth considering. Some people live in the same home for thirty years or more with no thought of ever leaving. Some people, after living in a place three or four years, feel the need to move on. The important question is whether there's a synergized commitment from both the occupant and the house.

One of my clients bought a small home after a prolonged and painful divorce. Marie spent a lot of money fixing it up and beautifying it both inside and out. I saw her several times during the first year she lived there, offering suggestions on bedroom setup, color ideas, and furniture placement. She turned it into a charming home for herself—a chance for her to heal. I felt a palpable resonance between her and this home, and felt hopeful she could get back on her feet. Since she lived in my neighborhood, I would drive by her home often and smile, thinking of how happy she was and how contented the house was.

A year after she completed all the work, Marie decided to sell it—just because. No other plans. She called me to come back with a new focus in mind: how to sell the house. I could hardly withstand the sadness the house was expressing. Even her cat had gotten sick. But she was committed to moving out. Marie agreed it was a nice place, affordable, reflected who she was, but she already had put money down on an apartment and was ready to be on her way. The house was on the market a year-and-a half before someone else bought it. Meanwhile, Marie was in a financial crisis trying to pay for both her apartment, which she moved into before the house sold, and her house. Here was a case of the house NOT being on board with the decision and not letting go.

However, if the home is prepared for a switch and the timing is right, and both occupant and home are committed to a change, typically, the home will sell within a reasonable time frame and with minimal glitches. Sometimes, the house has to take the lead to inform the owner it's time for a change to occur. If subtle hints don't work, the house may have to provide more overt cues. A friend of mine told me he hadn't thought about moving until four or five of his friends asked him about it. "When are you going to move from this place?" "Why don't you move into those new condos down by the river?" "Isn't it time for a change?" It got him to thinking. He moved.

Another client had someone show up at her door and simply offer to buy her place. It wasn't on the market and she hadn't given any thought to selling. But the offer was fair and, upon reflection, she was able to come up with a lot of valid reasons for why it would be appropriate to move at this time. After she was settled in her new place, she saw how beneficial it had been for her to change her environment. She never regretted it.

A student told me that she had been living in her apartment for about ten years when suddenly she began dreaming about moving. For the first few months, she thought it was a symbol about making changes in her life. But the dreams continued despite the fact she had changed her job and had come to terms with a difficult relationship. She took some major steps to improve her health, yet the moving dreams continued. One morning she woke up with the realization that the dreams meant moving-moving, not just changing circumstances. Within a week she was looking at condos and within a month was packing to move.

Sometimes your home has to take matters into its own "hands," so to speak . . .

Ellen and Jean were living together in a home which had been Ellen's originally for many years. When Jean moved in, they intended to stay there for many more years. Life went along fine for a while. They were both busy with careers and travel, so didn't have a lot of time to tune in to innuendoes that may be coming from the house. As with most people, they didn't even know they were supposed to be listening.

The issues started with the garage door. It stopped working. They called a repairman who supposedly fixed it, but the next evening when they came home from their respective jobs, it wouldn't open. The repairman was called twice more before they invested in a new door. They considered it lucky that their cars were never trapped in the garage. In hindsight, they saw the message that once they were out, they were prevented from getting back into their space.

Then one day Jean's key broke off in the lock to the front door. They didn't use the door that often so they figured the lock was old and got stuck. But a new lock didn't prevent the house from making itself heard. Jean and Ellen went through a spell of several weeks when one or the other would misplace their keys, or one of them would simply forget their keys, leaving them inside the house. In either case, they were locked out.

When the door knob to the front door fell off one day, that was the final piece that woke them up to what the house may be telling them. They began having conversations about moving and were surprised how easily the discussion took place between them. They both became enthused about looking for a new place to live—a place they could call "theirs." They've pondered the events leading up to their move and are committed to listening better should their new place begin dropping hints—or locking them out.

When you decide it's time to move, an appropriate action to take is to honor the place that you've called home for however long you were there. It deserves the respect of a goodbye, just as you would do with a dear friend. This could entail a couple of actions which are simple yet could make the difference between simply walking out the door or intentionally moving on. One action I suggest is to physically walk through your home. This can be done while you're still packing or you may do the walk-through just before the closing. You have the opportunity to look at the physical features with grateful eyes, remembering moments and events.

Another action to take is to write a goodbye letter to your home. This may not get done all in one sitting so allow enough time for you to say all you need to say. You may even find it necessary to write more than one goodbye letter: one to prepare the house for the upcoming change and the other just before the actual move-out. Despite the commitment both you and your home have made to this change, this doesn't mean there won't be some sadness, on both sides.

## Saying goodbye to your home

I. Get prepared.
Block off 30–40 minutes to do this exercise. Get a paper and pen—maybe some special stationery would be appropriate. You may want to light a candle, turn on some soft music, turn off the phone, and then breathe.

## 2. Final greeting

Start with Dear _____ inserting the name of your home or simply Dear Home. Feel the connection to your space as you do this. Wait until you feel everything's in place before you move on.

## 3. Thanks for the memories

Here are some ways to start your letter. Feel free to use other heartfelt ways to start your letter.

> You have been the best house for me because . . .
>
> Thank you for being here, especily while I . . .
> (or especially during . . .)
>
> I will miss you because . . .
>
> I will never forget you, especially because of . . .

## 4. Specific memories

Here is when you can outline a few "Do you remember when . . . ." events. List two or three that stand out in your mind.

## 5. The Best Features

Write down a couple of the features you loved the most about your home.

> The best part about you that I will never forget is . . .

It may be how much you loved the kitchen or how much you loved the backyard. You may decide your home's best feature was how charming it was.

## 6. Not always a picnic

There may be one or two problems the house presented to you during your time living there. If you feel drawn to do so, mention them here. It's okay to express your frustrations but be careful not to make them the main focus of the letter.

## 7. Assurance

Assure your home that you will be turning it over to someone who will care for it as much as you did. If you know of some changes they're planning to do to the home, now would be the time to mention those.

## 8. So Long

Write a final sign-off (Best of luck, Remembering you always, With fondness, etc.) and sign your name. If you've been keeping a scrapbook of your home, this letter would be the appropriate final entry. The other option is to take the letter outside and bury it on the property. Or you could put it in a red envelope and place it in a special place in your new home.

With a heartfelt closure ritual carried out for your old home, you are free to move forward to adventures with your new one. You would not be where you are today without the influence of this special place. Hold it dear in your heart as you begin another chapter in the "life of you" during which you will get to know and learn from another sacred home.

# Where to start?

A lot of exercises were presented in this section, some of which are more relevant to your life than others. It was never my intention that the you undertake all of them. If you are in the process of finding a new home, then the exercises in the Purpose stage would be appropriate. If you've recently moved into a place and are getting to know one another, then those in the Progression stage could fit your needs.

If you've lived in your home for several years or more, the Passion and Protection stages may present an exercise or two that would help you connect with your home. Finally, if you're thinking about moving, or have lost a home, the Parting stage may be suitable.

# Symbols of the Soul
## Archetypes

Physical forms are basically concentrated information—consciousness locked in specific patterns of awareness.

—*The Temple in the House*, Anthony Lawlor

Over the years, I have been invited into countless homes offering specific advice and actions to take to create a harmonious experience. I have listened to people's stories that started "ever since I moved in here . . ." and took note that a person's behavior changed in some way when they moved in—sometimes it was a positive change and sometimes it was negative.

Coincidental with this observation, a friend shared with me that the house next door to his kept attracting the same kind of people. When he and his family moved into the neighborhood, they soon discovered that their neighbors were reclusive. They would never join in on any of the neighborhood events and made no efforts to get to know anyone. When they moved, he and the other neighbors looked forward to a new family who might be more sociable. They were disappointed, however, when a young couple moved in and were also reclusive. Their stay was short-lived due to a transfer. To the amazement of the neighborhood, the third family kept to themselves as well, begging the question as to whether the house was influencing all these people in the same way.

I have had the unusual opportunity of working with clients who moved into a place where I had worked with the previous owners. One incident came about because my name was referred from one owner to the next. Others were completely serendipitous. Their stories started me thinking about the influence of homes in a different way.

In Feng Shui, it is not uncommon to see similar events that occur from one owner to the next: a couple gets divorced, the next couple who moves into their home gets divorced; a family is challenged financially, the next family who moves in is challenged financially as well. Sometimes, there's a third level of influence to another occupant of the space. These challenges seemed obviously triggered by something physical. A missing corner in the Partnership are of the house could account for the challenges in both relationships. A fireplace in the Wealth area of a home could account for money challenges in all who lived in the home.

From observing different people living in the same home, I was witnessing changes in behavioral patterns, however. There were no one or two physical attributes accounting for this change. It was as though the house as a whole was causing people to live in a different way and the new behavior was similar to those who lived in the space before them.

I worked with a couple who had lived in their home for several years. They were both quiet, studious, and appreciated a good intellectual conversation. They each had earned advanced degrees and worked in research. They sold their home to another couple who eventually called me to help them with the Feng Shui of their space. The new couple loved to entertain, but early on discovered that something always happened to prevent them from doing so—everything from an unexpected death in the family to a broken water pipe to an oven that experienced an untimely demise. They eventually, and intuitively, came to the conclusion that the house did not appreciate that kind of activity. Their love for this home informed their decision to forego any entertainment plans for awhile. Instead they took to having quiet evenings at home. Their behavior dramatically changed to accommodate what they felt was their home's preference.

In another situation, the wife was the main breadwinner in

the family and the husband stayed home with the children. He was happy to do so and enjoyed the close connection to the children. When she had a job opportunity somewhere else, they moved and sold their home to another family. Within the year, that wife had become the main source of income while her husband tended to their family after a job downsizing. Analyzing the costs of childcare and commuting expenses, they felt this was the best move for them. They were fully aware that a similar scenario had played out for the prior couple.

Observing these patterns got me thinking about whether we were dealing with coincidence or not or whether the structure itself was influencing the occupants in a way that was beyond what I had been targeting as a Feng Shui consultant.

I searched through my Feng Shui books to see if anyone else was verifying these patterns, but I found no reference to them. I took more and more notice of the phenomenon that there were certain energies a house would hold all on its own. This energy seemed to contribute to why a person may like their home or why they may not do well in a home. I spoke to my colleagues in the Feng Shui world about what I was observing but it was hard to describe and felt nebulous. They all agreed that though a house could indeed hold its own unique energy, no one had developed the idea.

Because I was noticing specific patterns playing out in people's lives, I started to recognize them. They became identifiable so, just as I advise people name their homes, I decided to name the patterns. They became archetypes. Carl Jung coined the term "archetype" ("arche" means *first*, and "type" means *kind—first of its kind*) and defined them as universally recognized patterns. An archetype employs a language of symbolic behavior that will provide a probable and typical outcome in a situation. By understanding archetypes, you can better understand a character in a movie, a friend's actions, or a puzzling situation.

An archetype can be described as an ideal model or stereotype (like *mother* or *hero* or *achiever*)—all terms we understand. Yet there is always a dark side to these archetypes. A *mother* can become *controller;* the *hero* could switch over to the *martyr;* or the *achiever* could become the *driver.* It is not enough to identify the archetype, it is also necessary to determine whether it is in its ideal form or exaggerated form. It is then possible to predict corresponding results.

Adhering to the concept that all created forms have conscious energy, a building or home would accommodate the archetype construct. There are those who can read the historical layers of land; there are others who can read the behavioral patterns of animals; gardeners who acknowledge that the vitality within their plants increases when they connect with them on a regular basis. Our homes are waiting to be recognized too. I have identified nine possible archetypes based on the principles of the Taoist calendar, the Feng Shui compass, and the Chinese Five Elements:

> Magician
> Adaptor
> Protector
> Visionary
> Realist
> Advocate
> Director

Innovator

Mystic

Knowing the underlying archetype of your home can help you offset its natural tendencies if those tendencies may be negative for you. If the archetype is beneficial to you, its features can be maximized.

## How to determine your home's archetype

One way to determine the pattern your home may be expressing is due to the time-span during which it was built. Subscribing to the theory that a space is alive and therefore susceptible to outside factors, the period of time during which a home was constructed can provide some insight into its basic archetypal nature. A building or home would not be immune to the influences of its environment. It stands to reason a structure built during a time of chaos may take on some of the surrounding chaos.

Likewise, a home built during economic stress could always have a hint of that tone in its walls. On the other hand, a building put up during a relatively prosperous and peaceful time in history will likewise have that tendency. Although this archetypal information is broad and basic, it may explain some central theme you seem to be experiencing in your life. Based on the date of construction, the corresponding archetypes are.

1844–1863—Magician
1864–1883—Adaptor
1884–1903—Protector
1904–1923—Visionary

1924–1943—Realist
1944–1963—Advocate
1964–1983—Director
1984–2003— Innovator
2004–2023—Mystic

*See Addendum A: Explanation for Age of House for more information about the significance and background of the year.*

It must be understood that the sweeping generality of using construction dates to determine the archetype of your home doesn't account for other factors that could influence it. Although your home may begin with one archetype, that archetype could change.

An archetype can be changed by the people who sequentially occupy the space. Just as we are all influenced by the people we meet, a space will be influenced by the occupants who come through its doors. The challenges or the blessings they bring to the house could override its innate predisposition. The house may have had to adapt to accommodate the occupants' preferences. A home that was built during a time of celebration and expansion but occupied by people who are more comfortable with a quiet and more introverted lifestyle can make some adaptations over time to better fit the tendencies of the current occupants. This adjustment is not without problems and can account for the occupants feeling like something is just not right until the revised archetype is in place.

The other way a space's natural inclination may be changed is by a dramatic remodel. This would have to involve a change in the footprint of the space or a change in the roof line. It's also possible to change the basic energy of the space when the remodeling involves the bedrooms and the kitchen. Such a massive physical transformation enables the house to be re-formed and re-shaped, with the intention of moving more in line with the current occupants.

### Archetype questionnaire

As you can see, combining the date of construction, factoring in the history of the predecessors, and taking into consideration any significant remodeling, a home can not only change its archetype but may have a strong pattern in place before you even move in. The questionnaire that follows, Discovering the Archetype of Your Home, will help you determine more specifically which of nine possible archetypes your home may be exhibiting.

It's possible that your home will have more than one archetype. If you have two that are tied for first place or one that is a very close second, read about both archetypes. In fact, your home may incorporate two or three of the nine archetypes. Just as individuals are an amalgam of various characteristics, your home may be as well. It's also possible that two people who live in the same house will get different archetypes because a home relates differently to different people. Just as I may be more direct and forthright with an employee, but more gentle and flexible with a family member, a home may also adjust its approach with individuals based on their needs.

Once you've determined your archetype(s), refer to the appropriate section in the book to read specifics about it. You will find a description of each of the archetypes and stories of how the archetype might play out in real life. There is also a section giving you suggestions on the best way to connect with your archetype in a personal and intimate way. The reason you may want to connect is to seek advice, to express concerns, or just to get to know your home better.

If you feel you are not well-matched to your archetype, read the section about challenges that could occur with that particular home along with a Feng Shui adjustment to help ease any issues. You can consider this a negotiation between you and your home to help harmonize the relationship without having to go through an enormous remodeling project, or feeling the need to move.

Finally, each archetype provides some words of advice from the *I Ching*. These are meant for you to ponder not only in terms of your home but also your own life. If the particular phrase from your archetype doesn't make sense to you, stay with it for a while as you will eventually get clarity as to how it applies.

In line with the premise of this book, which says that your space is alive and vibrant, it would also be entirely appropriate to ask your home what archetype it is and let it guide you to the right one. You can use the date of construction and the questionnaire as a guide but use your intuition for the final archetype confirmation.

# Discovering the Archetype of Your Home Questionnaire

Please use the rating scale below to complete the boxes on each page. Choose the rating from 0 to 5 that seems closest to the description of your situation. Be honest and go with the first answer that comes to you.

0 – No/Never

1 – Seldom/Not Much

2 – Sometimes

3 – Usually

4 – Yes

5 – Strongly Agree/Definite Yes

Add up all the total numbers in the columns and then transfer those numbers to the last page. The highest number is the archetype of your home.

## GROUP I

| | 1 | 2 | 3 |
|---|---|---|---|
| There is a continual flow of people and/or events in my house. | ____ | | |
| My house easily accommodates both large and small groups. | | ____ | |
| This house has been in the family for many generations. | | | ____ |
| I live in a place that is entertainment central for huge events. | ____ | | |
| Sometimes my home feels very private although not exclusive. | | ____ | |
| I feel my house nurtures me. | | | ____ |
| I am intimidated in my home. | ____ | | |
| My house has looked the same for as long as I can remember. | | ____ | |
| My house feels like it keeps me stuck in the past. | | | ____ |
| TOTAL COLUMN 1 | ____ | | |
| TOTAL COLUMN 2 | | ____ | |
| TOTAL COLUMN 3 | | | ____ |

## GROUP 2

| Statement | 4 | 5 | 6 |
|---|---|---|---|
| Living in this house, I feel like I have a new idea every day. | ____ | | |
| I like the practical and efficient layout of my home. | | ____ | |
| My house feels strong and sturdy. | | | ____ |
| Sometimes life is hectic and chaotic in this house. | ____ | | |
| Since I've been living here, I am careful how I spend my money. | | ____ | |
| Everyone feels at home in my house. | | | ____ |
| When I moved in, my life took a dramatic turn. | ____ | | |
| Living in this house, I draw money to me easily. | | ____ | |
| I enjoy working out of my home. | | | ____ |
| TOTAL COLUMN 4 | ____ | | |
| TOTAL COLUMN 5 | | ____ | |
| TOTAL COLUMN 6 | | | ____ |

|  | 7 | 8 | 9 |
|---|---|---|---|

## GROUP 3

Since living in my house, I consider
myself an independent thinker. _____ (7)

I have quirky and unique things
in my home. _____ (8)

There is a spiritual, sacred quality
in my home. _____ (9)

My home really likes order and
organization. _____ (7)

I have an eclectic mix of furnishings. _____ (8)

I'm always trying to use green or
natural products in my house. _____ (9)

I feel like my home does not do well
with a lot of confusion. _____ (7)

I love high-quality items, but worry
about being materialistic. _____ (8)

My house makes me feel like I might
be rather rigid in my thinking. _____ (9)

TOTAL COLUMN 7 _____

TOTAL COLUMN 8 _____

TOTAL COLUMN 9 _____

|  | 10 | 11 | 12 |
|---|---|---|---|

## GROUP 4

My house seems haunted. ___ (10)

I love hosting family holidays. ___ (11)

A gathering at my house isn't complete without children. ___ (12)

Some of the details in my house make it feel elaborate. ___ (10)

Since living in my home, I often feelas though I'm going in many directions. ___ (11)

One of my greatest pleasures is cooking in my kitchen. ___ (12)

When people drive by, they always notice my home. ___ (10)

When I'm at home, it's hard for me to make decisions. ___ (11)

When people come to my house, they gather in the kitchen. ___ (12)

TOTAL COLUMN 10 ___

TOTAL COLUMN 11 ___

TOTAL COLUMN 12 ___

144

|  | 13 | 14 | 15 |
|---|---|---|---|

## GROUP 5

Since living in my home, I have
been open to new adventures.
_____ (13)

I don't mind working quietly
by myself at home.
_____ (14)

Sometimes I like to have a quiet
afternoon where I just stay home.
_____ (15)

At times I feel there are too many
possibilities.
_____ (13)

Simplicity best describes my life.
_____ (14)

I feel my house is not allowing me
to move forward in my life.
_____ (15)

My lifestyle is very active and
athletic.
_____ (13)

I feel lethargic, discouraged at
home
_____ (14)

I've been very financially successful
since living in this home.
_____ (15)

TOTAL COLUMN 13 _____

TOTAL COLUMN 14 _____

TOTAL COLUMN 15 _____

|  | 16 | 17 | 18 |
|---|---|---|---|

## GROUP 6

I love having adequate space for
my books.
_____ (16)

When I'm home alone, I tend to worry
too much about what others think.
_____ (17)

When I'm home, I'm frequently
thinking about my life's purpose.
_____ (18)

I'm pretty methodical and regular about
tending to things around my house.
_____ (16)

I feel I've accomplished a lot since
living in my home.
_____ (17)

There is a peaceful simplicity about
my house.
_____ (18)

When I'm home, I have less tolerance
for clutter than I do anywhere else.
_____ (16)

When I'm home by myself I sometimes
wonder where I get these innovative
ideas.
_____ (17)

It's important to me tonurture my
spiritual side.
_____ (18)

    TOTAL COLUMN 16    _____

    TOTAL COLUMN 17    _____

    TOTAL COLUMN 18    _____

Total your scores for each column and enter them in the spaces below to determine the archetype of your home.

Col. 1 _____ + Col. 10 _____ = _____ Magician

Col. 2 _____ + Col. 11 _____ = _____ Adapter

Col. 3 _____ + Col. 12 _____ = _____ Protector

Col. 4 _____ + Col. 13 _____ = _____ Visionary

Col. 5 _____ + Col. 14 _____ = _____ Realist

Col. 6 _____ + Col. 15 _____ = _____ Advocate

Col. 7 _____ + Col. 16 _____ = _____ Director

Col. 8 _____ + Col. 17 _____ = _____ Innovator

Col. 9 _____ + Col. 18 _____ = _____ Mystic


List the top two highest scores to determine your home's archetype.

#1 _____ Archetype _____

#2 _____ Archetype _____


Turn to the appropriate pages in the book to read about the archetypes and gain insight regarding the tendencies of where you live!

> We need a home to shore up our states of mind,
> to compensate for our vulnerabilities, because so
> much of the world is opposed to our allegiances. We
> need our rooms to align us to desirable versions of
> ourselves and to keep alive the important, evanes-
> cent sides of us.
>
> —*The Architecture of Happiness,* Alain de Botton

# MAGICIAN ARCHETYPE

Homes built in the era of the Magician capture an expressive energy. It is not uncommon for these homes to be built with a lot of ornamentation along with a bit of ostentation. The Magician brings with it the audacity that is needed to make the leap from tradition to a new way of thinking. There is a fearless self-assurance that emanates from a Magician home. Its strength and power can motivate seeds of possibility in those who live within its walls.

The Magician archetype home is a catalyst for supporting situations or people who need to change. It is a natural alchemist, blending and mixing seemingly incongruent and unrelated parts into a final amalgam of excitement and panache. The Magician home likes nothing more than supporting change and expansion of its occupants, and may often provide situations that would normally be uncomfortable for those who live there. Having to host a fund-raising event or a charity gala is right up the alley of the Magician home, often ignoring the level of discomfort that may be coming from the owners who want to live a less public lifestyle.

Its independence and free spirit keep it from doting on the occupants in a protective and nurturing way. Although always aware of their reactions, the Magician's intent is to stretch and broaden their horizons regardless of their discomfort. Furthermore, its lavish style and gregarious nature would never be held down by the concerns and fears of the owners.

The Magician archetype appreciates a continual flow of friends and acquaintances, mostly to show off its striking qualities. It gladly takes on the title of being the "entertainment center." Although it can put forth an elegant gesture for a small gathering, the Magician really shines when hosting a large event—the larger the better. Some of the events may be public while others may take on a more private feel, like a wedding reception or an anniversary party. It opens wide its doors, welcomes people into its grand entry and lets them mingle and flow amidst beautiful surroundings and bountiful food.

Due to its social nature, the Magician home may even welcome in spirits; it is not uncommon for a Magician structure to be haunted. Because it is just the kind of place that reaches out in all directions, a misplaced entity or two will always be welcome in this space. It only adds enticement and mystery to its character. Even if the ghosts have been cleared, the Magician house will see to it others can find their way in to keep the thrill going.

The Magician is very particular about its appearance. Like a spoiled child used to getting its way, this home does not settle for second best and will find ways for cheap carpeting to have to be replaced or the sale-bought fixture to hit the floor. It lends itself naturally to a gingerbread look with ornate woodwork and embellished details. It's one of the few archetypes that has the majesty and style to pull off the elaborate style.

This archetype does not do well when it is split up into individual living areas. Many Magician homes are large which lends itself well to cutting the space into three or four separate apartments for economic reasons. This is not an agreeable arrangement with the Magician who will often find a way to prevent it from happening by mischievous occurrences that eventually cause the owner to give up the idea. A broken water-pipe, a disappearing contractor, permit issues can all derail the project, leaving the owner to say it "was just not meant to be."

If, however, the project *does* take place, it wouldn't be unlike a Magician to see that the individual tenants are unhappy or struggling in some way. Because if everyone moved out, the space could possibly be returned to its former glory and resume its magical façade, as happened in the following story.

### Florence's story

Florence moved into a small apartment that had been con-verted from a large home. When she went to look at the apart-ment the first time, she was struck by the size and majesty of the house. However, for financial reasons, the owners had converted the entire space into six apartments. Florence was charmed by the place and signed a three-year lease.

A year later she was looking for a way to get out of her lease. Her life was not going well financially or physically. Her health had deteriorated so that she was barely able to keep her job as a dietician. Besides that, all the other tenants had moved out so the place was empty. This made for some tense moments when Florence would hear noises at night or hear someone walking outside her door. Not only did this disrupt her sleep but her sense of security.

The entire year Florence lived in the space, she could not determine which room was actually her bedroom. Although one of the rooms made sense, it didn't feel right. It was obvious that it used to be a parlor and she could not reconcile the parlor energy with that required of a bedroom. There was a room that was probably a bedroom in the original design of the house, but it was too close to the entry door to her apartment and she felt vulnerable. She had moved her bed back and forth between the two rooms three times in the year that she lived there, hoping to find a place that would work.

Eventually, Florence was able to leave and moved to another apartment, where her health improved immediately and she was slept better. The owners of the house were forced to sell their property. Over the next six months, the new owners made major repairs both inside and out. The house was returned to its original intent as a single-family home. It became the focal point of the neighborhood with its strong, handsome presence. Purchased by two successful musicians, it became the hub of musical recitals and small opera performances—in true Magician fashion.

It's best that those who are living in a Magician home love to entertain, and in a big way. Their lives may be community-focused, enabling them to offer their home for various activities. It is the perfect place for someone who is an activist and a forward-thinker, to match the active energy coming from the space.

**How to talk to the Magician home:** If you want to reach the Magician home in a personal and intimate way, the best approach is a first-class one. Writing a letter to your home in a special journal which was purchased for just this purpose and using a new pen will please the most particular Magician. It loves ritual so lighting a candle would be appropriate or bringing flowers to the table would be a nice touch. It also loves galas so having decadent chocolate along with a glass of wine could open the channels.

Don't expect to rush through the process. The Magician wants things done in a particular way, with ceremony and grace. You will find that once you express your intention to honor the Magician's exquisite tastes and attention to detail, it will be more than happy to communicate. In fact, you may have a very ready and willing participant with the Magician archetype.

**Challenges to occupants:** Over-confidence may be exhibited by the Magician home, making some occupants feel intimidated and overwhelmed. The magical catalytic tendencies of the Magician can become those of a trickster, playing games with the occupants or visitors. The Magician archetype home is known for its unexplained events, which may cause occupants to feel uneasy and threatened. It is best not to get caught up in any emotional turmoil that may be going on in the powerful and playful Magician home.

**Feng Shui action to take:** In order to offset the impulsive nature that can occur with the Magician archetype, the space must reflect a grounded and anchored message. An effective adjustment is to install a brick walkway leading up to the front door, the brick acting as an anchor for any high-flying tendencies. Another way to get the same effect is to install marble on the inside entry floor. Either way, the message is about walking firmly and steadily on the earth.

**Message of the Magician archetype:** Be content in your home and joyful in the way you live.

# ADAPTER ARCHETYPE

*Matt's adaptive house*

Matt bought his first home from a retired couple who were planning to move to warmer climates. They had raised 4 children in the small home; Matt was single and already had a room-mate to help with the mortgage payment.

For the first couple of years, the two guys lived together, coming and going with their own lives. They each had their own room and managed the shared areas without a problem. Their third year together Matt, who had been working for an investment firm, decided to quit and start his own business. He set up his office in the basement. He had it refinished and upgraded to make the space comfortable and efficient. His room-mate meanwhile got married and moved out. Matt found someone else to take the space but not before moving his office upstairs. His new room-mate had the basement.

Matt's business did very well for the next few years, necessitating an employee. He managed this arrangement for a year or two then decided to move his business out of his house to a bigger, more professional space. For a few months, another friend crashed at Matt's home sleeping in the room that was the office.

When business slowed down, Matt was in a position to move his office back to his basement because that room-mate had decided to take a job out East. Eventually Matt got engaged and married and moved his business back out of the house. His wife loved his home, appreciating its versatility and adaptability over the years. They lived there for five more years and moved after the birth of their second child.

The Adapter is the most compliant archetype, shifting and adjusting to the activities and personalities of the occupants. One day it can be the center of a huge event and the next will beautifully and gracefully host a small tea party. The specific strength of the Adapter archetype is being able to adapt and flow with the people who live within its walls. It's as though it takes its identity from the occupants.

Its adaptability, however, implies an inherent strength. Although it does accommodate beautifully and may seem to "go with the flow," it still has a strong presence and a strong sense of direction to support and guide the occupants. The Adapter home offers solid footing in the form of consistency, tenacity, and determination that reflects on the occupants at the right moment.

Unlike the Magician, the Adapter archetype is able to appreciate a more intimate lifestyle and a sense of privacy. Although the entrances to these homes may still be somewhat grand, they are scaled back from those of the Magician. In some cases, the Adapter entrances are not obvious at all or may be down-played. Typically there are fewer front windows than the Magician requires, indicating an ability to disconnect from the world when needed.

The Adapter archetype extends an "all things to all people" vibration. It provides occupants an opportunity to maintain their equilibrium while they move in directions they may not have considered before. Although there may be a lot of shuffling and re-arranging (of people, job situations, furniture, room designation, etc.), there is a steadiness and innate balance that is indisputable. The Adapter supports change and even new ways of thinking yet upholds and reflects common sense.

The message of flexibility is particularly relevant when it

comes to business. Whether operating the business inside or outside the walls of the Adapter, occupants will be able to tap into the strength behind this archetype enabling them to ride out the sometimes erratic movement inherent to any kind of venture. The Adapter contributes clear focus despite distractions and the ability to course-correct as needed, assuring the occupants of career success.

Intuitive people are well-supported by the Adapter home since it can accommodate their imaginative explorations. Likewise, writers and artists find this setting conducive to the highs and lows of their creative process.

**How to talk to the Adapter archetype:** If you live in an Adapter home, you do not have to stand on ceremony in order to connect. Pretty much anything will go. However, as a token of respect, ringing a small brass bell or windchime before writing or speaking to your home would be appropriate. The sound of the bell will gently draw the Adapter's attention your way.

Once you feel you have its attention, don't be surprised if it expects you to draw your message, rather than write it. Have some colored pencils on hand just in case the communication goes in this direction. The Adapter is not looking for artwork, but more your feeling, so don't be intimidated. Some soft music in the background would draw in your archetype. The sound of water from a fountain or water sounds on a CD will entice as well.

The Adapter is a gentle, sweet spirit that will love to talk about your journey with you. It may have some business advice that would be helpful if you can tune in. Keep in mind, this archetype will not be offended in the least if you simply don't make contact. But it will be worth it if you can take on some of its tenacity and be persistent in establishing a relationship.

**Challenges to occupants:** If the changeable nature of the Adapter home gets out of control, the home becomes over-accommodating, even vulnerable. At this point, the occupants may find themselves going in various directions and unable to focus. They may be unable to make a decision and may find themselves drowning in their frenzy.

**Feng Shui action to take:** To keep the Adapter archetype in balance, it is necessary to add a symbolic reminder that will soak up the excess flow of energy. It is best to place a live green plant near the front door, a potent and pivotal spot according to Feng Shui principles. The plant will not only represent the action of reining in over-abundant current, but also the need to nurture and grow.

**Message of the Adapter archetype:** Be firm and clear, but do not provoke or dazzle.

> Returning home at the end of the day, we can slowly resume contact with a more authentic self, who was there waiting in the wings for us to end our performance.
>
> —*The Architecture of Happiness,* Alain de Botton

## PROTECTOR ARCHETYPE

The Protector archetype has a kind and loving energy, making it a great family home. It supports both the young and the old: the growth of children as well as the nurturance required for older family members. This archetype holds an inherent sense of stability and steadiness. It is not uncommon for generation after generation of the same family to live within its walls. Despite difficult family dynamics that may have occurred while growing up, family members often look forward to return visits because of the fond memories of the home itself. They miss the experience of living under the protection of such a dear old friend.

The Protector home gladly opens its doors wide to any entertainment opportunities, large or small, especially if family is involved. It appreciates the constant flow of activities, no matter what the motive, as long as the space is being used in an upright and honest way, without ostentation or a show of extravagance. Hosting family holidays is a favorite activity of the Protector. It truly appreciates the presence of children and offers them many great playtime opportunities. If the family isn't graced with their own children or only a few, the home entices other children to come in—neighbor kids, relatives, friends of their children.

There's a lot of innate nurturance in a Protector home. It's a place where healing can take place, both physically and emotionally. The kitchen is usually near the center of this kind of home and operates as the hub and gathering place day and night. A Protector home is happiest when the aroma of freshly baked bread is permeating the space. It's a place where wounded hearts can be mended and shy hearts can open up. The enticement of cookies and tea around the kitchen table can bring most people to a place of wholeness and a place of "home."

Because of the Protector's need to nourish on so many levels, it is important that it have a direct connection to nature. Often, there is a garden just outside the back door—vegetable, herb, flower or a combination of all of them. Tending to the garden and being in touch with the natural cycle of the seasons protects the occupants from the frenzy of day-to-day life and provides a balance to a hectic lifestyle. The Protector likes to be considered a small piece of heaven here on earth.

This is a great home for large families or people who are starting a family—where the children energy is high and abundant. People who like to cook and maybe even raise their own food will find the Protector archetype a perfect match. The Protector home does well in the country but will also thrive in the city, as long as there's land around the space.

### Jenny vs. the Protector

Jenny lived in the same house all her life, the youngest of five children. Her memories growing up were of her mother in the kitchen. Although she had a part-time job, Allie made sure she was home when her kids returned from school each day. She also made it clear that they could bring home any of their classmates at any time—there would always be an after-school treat. Jenny remembered many fun times spent in the kitchen with her mom and her friends as well as her siblings' friends. And, more than once, Allie would pull up extra chairs for supper for those who didn't want to go home, as there was always plenty to eat.

Jenny also remembered the extensive garden that her mom and dad had created in the backyard. Most weekends found them there weeding, planting, harvesting. Allie was known for her homemade soups and was proud when she could say that most of the ingredients came from her garden. She shared her secret recipes with her daughters and gave all her kids some lessons on planting their own small garden.

After high school, Jenny decided not to go to college right

away. She was unsure where her interests were going and decided to get clear. All of her other brothers and sisters had moved out of the house, but none of them had moved very far away. Most of them stopped by each day to see what was cooking, literally. Meanwhile, Jenny took a job at a local bookstore working part-time and living at home.

As the years past, Jenny began to feel unsettled. Her friends were graduating from college and making their way in the world. Jenny was still in the room in which she grew up and still working at the bookstore. When one of her best friends graduated, got married and had a baby, Jenny realized her life had somehow stopped. Suddenly the walls were closing in on her and she needed to find a way out. Her father had passed away suddenly a few years before and since she was the last one at home, she felt the need to stay with her mother. This worked fine, for a while. The first few conversations Jenny had with Allie about starting college and moving out were painful. Although not wanting to hold her back, Allie already felt the loss and the emptiness.

Jenny did move out, however, completed her degree in an accelerated program, and began her own life in her own space. Her mother continues to live in the house by herself, still cooks huge quantities of food and still feeds whoever walks in the door. Any suggestion she move to a smaller home results in no change.

**How to speak to the Protector:** The Protector archetype appreciates food and flowers. Having a bouquet of fresh-cut flowers as opposed to a formal arrangement is best. A plate of homemade cookies or some fresh-baked muffins—something sweet—opens the channel to the Protector. As is customary, you can feel free to indulge yourself during your writing or while you're tuning in to your home. After all, the Protector likes nothing more than to nourish.

The Protector home appreciates live music, so if you're inclined to play the piano or strum a guitar, or even sing a song, you will be met with open arms. Putting on recorded music won't do much for this archetype so, without live music, it's best to provide a quiet time with no distractions. Sitting near a window, out on a patio, or in your garden would offer a connection to nature and may provide you some discussion opportunities with your archetype.

Keep in mind the Protector does that—protects. It is not a big risk-taker. It may have a tendency to worry and will advise accordingly, wanting to keep you safe. That said, it will always have your best interests at heart and will listen patiently trying to see your side of things. It will comfort as you cry; it will hold you as you heal. There could not be a better confidante than the Protector archetype.

**Challenges to occupants:** The Protector archetype loves being a guardian, but in doing so may become very controlling. People living in a Protector home may get stuck in the past or may be slow to integrate changes. A Protector archetype can become over-protective, thereby bogging down the occupants who find it difficult to move forward.

**Feng Shui action to take:** When a rug gets trampled down, we shake it out. When a pillow gets mashed down, we fluff it up. When a house gets stuck, we stir it up in someway as well. A metal wind-chime hung near the front entry will assure a continual movement and flow in the lives of those who live there.

**Message of the Protector archetype:** Be the mother power that guides but does not control, gives but does not claim.

## VISIONARY ARCHETYPE

The Visionary home holds a lot of vitality and a lot of spark. Upon first moving in, occupants may feel energized and inclined to take on a whole new direction in their lives. However, the energy of this archetype isn't gradual and it doesn't provide an easy transition. Instead, you could liken it to being hit by lightning. There is a strong-willed drive behind the Visionary home that stops at nothing. Projects get started, ideas get generated, new ventures are planned—possibilities and opportunities abound. Living in a Visionary archetype can reflect a forward-thinking and can-do attitude.

Without dramatic details and frills, this archetype emphasizes efficiency and simplicity. The physical layout of the Visionary home may even be simple to underscore its preference. Eliminating outward frills and details in its physical appearance mirrors the need to eliminate distractions. The Visionary is very focused. For this reason, having a home-based business in a Visionary home is very appropriate, depending on the nature of the business. It would not work if the business is massage or therapy where a quieter, gentler energy would be best. However, someone who is in sales could find this active energy to be quite beneficial.

The Visionary home is all about action and doing. It thrives on witnessing productivity in its occupants. However, due to its rash nature there may be just as many crashes as successes, but this does not daunt the Visionary archetype. The thrill of starting over and finding new ways to maneuver through difficulties is part of the make-up of this energy. Earning and losing large sums of money is part of the process to the Visionary energy—it's all about the push forward and the thrill of the gamble.

This is a home for high-energy people who prosper from lots of activity. Those who are athletic or active physically can benefit from the intensity of the Visionary.

### Joe and Ellie and the boys

Joe and Ellie lived in a home with their three teen-age boys. They had moved to this home two years prior when their youngest turned 10 to accommodate their growing needs. Their life was built around hockey. All three sons played in various leagues and Joe coached one of his son's hockey teams. Hockey trophies and equipment permeated their place. Ellie relished the high energy of her "4 boys" and actively participated in this lifestyle, shuttling kids around, attending games, and cheering them on to victory.

Their home from a Feng Shui perspective offered many glaring challenges that, under normal circumstances, would have been concerning. One of the issues was that they lived in a split-entry home. This situation occurs at the front door when a half-flight of stairs leads to the basement and another half-flight of stairs leads to the main living area. A split-entry home sets up a potential pattern of confusion since a decision about "where to go" is a continual message at the entrance. A round rug in the entry could help to ease that message, but Joe and Ellie didn't have one.

Second, all of the family bedrooms were located in a projection located out in front of the front door. When this occurs there can be division between a couple and/or between family members due to the disconnect and the distance from the main entrance where energy enters the space. A mirror in the back half of the house can "pull" the bedrooms back behind the door, but there was no such mirror in their home.

Finally, they were all sleeping over the three-car garage which creates a potential for physical and emotional issues. A garage, although enclosed and sometimes heated, does not provide the support needed for a good night's sleep. There is a potential for fatigue, stress, and low energy when sleeping over a garage. Placing a mirror under the bed or rocks in each of the corners would help ground the occupants, however, Joe and Ellie didn't know to do this.

It goes without saying that the clutter and turmoil reflected in the lifestyle of this family was enormous. Because of rhe active and busy lives of their sons and their corresponding involvement, Joe and Ellie did not pay attention to the details. Although they wished they could keep their home picked up and in order, it wasn't happening. Clutter filled every corner and every countertop.

Yet, despite all these potential challenges, they were the picture of health, seemingly well-balanced, and fun-loving. They were a close-knit group, spent as much time together as they could, and dreaded the day when the oldest son would leave for college. When they weren't involved in hockey, they went hiking in the Rockies or white-water rafting in Oregon. What would account for their happy healthy lives under such Feng Shui-adverse living conditions? How could they be overriding all these challenges? Having a Visionary home could be the reason. Thriving on excitement and the thrill of action and challenges, the energy of their home may be the only explanation for their active, outgoing way of life.

**How to speak to the Visionary:** The Visionary is probably going to want you to dance your way into communication. Movement and physical action is in line with how a Visionary responds. Drumming is another way to align with your archetype. A candle and some flowers will just not be the key to opening up the door.

The Visionary can provide some great ideas as to how to get something started in your life. If you're living in a Visionary home, chances are you're being asked to make a drastic change in your life. This is the perfect archetype to help you do that and will provide you ample opportunities to get out of your rut.

Unlike the Protector, the Visionary blossoms when there is a chance of risk. It can provide an agile and quick-thinking environment for your home and for your business. It is creative and inventive, providing ample ideas for a new venture or a new brainchild.

**Challenges to occupants:** Living in a Visionary home can be exhausting for those people who are looking for a calm place to hang their hat. There is the possibility that when events get increasingly more vigorous and energetic, the Visionary may become unfocused. Too many things going on, too much activity, too many possibilities can all be indicative that the Visionary archetype is out of balance. There is a tendency to overwhelm.

If someone has a propensity to be unorganized, a Visionary home may magnify this predisposition. It will be important for those living there to maintain a plan of discipline in order to keep moving forward yet not get lost in indecision.

**Feng Shui action to take:** When activities are spinning out of control, adding an item that will be a symbol of balance, stability, and focus is the key. A round rug, a round table, a round lamp, a piece of round art placed in the bedroom can counteract the dizzying effects of the Visionary archetype when it has taken on too many things.

**Message of the Visionary archetype:** See clearly and act with tranquility.

> Where we love is home—home that our feet may
> leave but not our hearts. —Oliver Wendell Holmes

## REALIST ARCHETYPE

*Uncle Ted and his money*

Ted's nieces and nephews were stunned to discover he was a multi-millionaire. Even though he was 80, he had died unexpectedly in a car crash on his way to visit a friend in a nursing home. His next of kin were recipients of his inheritance, unaware that he would be leaving each of them with a life-changing amount of money.

Uncle Ted and Aunt Helen had always been dear people. Their love and generosity over the years extended to their five nieces and nephews without question, since they never had children of their own. Uncle Ted worked for the government right after World War II for about 25 years. He took an early retirement and then started his own business as a contract specifications writer for architectural firms. He had his drafting table and resource library set up in the basement of their home and spent many quiet hours down there by himself.

When Aunt Helen was alive, she would tell stories about how over the years he had become so frugal—saving string, not throwing away rubber bands, keeping empty glass jars. In the early part of their marriage, she remembered him as a carefree kind of guy, spending money on her and trips they took as a young couple. As they settled into their home and their life, Ted talked about the need to save. They had never owned a new car and had paid off their mortgage years ago. Their relatives assumed they were struggling to make ends meet. What they didn't know was that Ted was making some wise and careful investments, netting them huge sums of money.

Uncle Ted's relatives wondered if Aunt Helen even knew just exactly how much they had since Ted handled all the money, making decisions on how and when to make their big purchases. Any visitors to the house remember Ted diligently sitting at his desk in the basement working on "something" day after day. No one asked any questions since he seemed contented.

This is the story of a man aligning with his home's innate tendencies to be focused, practical, and successful—which clearly brought out his own corresponding predisposition.

Those living in a Realist home can expect a less frenetic experience than that of the Visionary. Like the Visionary home, frills and excess are not characteristics of this archetype; a simpler physical environment creates a simpler lifestyle. Rather, an occupant is more likely to find the qualities of reliability, dependability, and responsibility lurking amid the walls. The Realist is very clear about a direction and steadily applies itself to that end. It doesn't get lost in distractions or isn't apt to follow the latest trend. Instead, it's steady as she goes.

166

It doesn't mean the Realist archetype lacks any excitement or joy. In fact, this home is very adept at enticing success and prosperity through the door. Those living in a Realist home have the potential for bringing in wealth yet without the ostentation often associated with people who make a lot of money. Often these people are labeled "the millionaire next door" where they quietly and modestly live their lives, meanwhile amassing a fortune in investments. There is no outward evidence of their net worth because of their practical and simple lifestyle. Their experience of accomplishment and joy comes from fostering this secret that is usually known by only a few individuals.

Occupants who are well-suited for this Realist experience have the perseverance and long-term vision to understand the payoffs in the end. Their spending habits are modest; in fact, despite their financial resources, the occupants buy used cars and household items that are on sale. Only when it matters deeply to them will they spend lavishly, like on a special piece of art or gold jewelry. These purchases are still in line with their spending motivation since they could be considered investments.

This archetype is a perfect setting for those who have the discipline along with the vision and tenacity to start their own business. Realist homes can foster self-made millionaires whether the business is actually in the home or somewhere else. Its influence will be felt on the occupants regardless of where they actually do their work.

**How to speak to the Realist:** As you might imagine, the Realist will not be impressed with a lavish approach. If you're living with a Realist archetype, keep it simple when doing this exercise, otherwise, the connection will not be very successful.

The Realist does have a softer, intuitive side, but is less comfortable tapping into that aspect. It would be best to approach the Realist with a practical question rather than just having an experience. If it's about business, all the better. Once the channels have been opened, you can delicately address more sensitive matters.

Native American flute music works well as an invitation to this archetype because of its simple melody lines. A jade plant or some bamboo should be the extent of "décor" elements— again simple and straightforward. Don't expect a warm and tender connection at first; the Realist needs to be eased into communicating on a level other than practical matters. However, you will find it very rewarding if you can call forth from within yourself the innate Realist traits of tenacity and perseverance. Your home will recognize and appreciate your efforts.

**Challenges to occupants:** Because the Realist archetype is practical and economical, the challenge that could occur is that it has a tendency to be sluggish or discouraged. Someone living or working in this space may find it hard not to become lethargic. Overcome by fear of extravagance or a concern for being irresponsible, the occupants hang back and avoid decisions that could be in their best interest.

**Feng Shui action to take:** In order to overcome the exaggerated version of the Realist archetype, the home needs to incorporate an element of drama. Adding red to the front door, painting a room red, or incorporating the color red in artwork can all off-set the stagnation, bringing the home and its occupants back to a balanced Realist position.

**Message of the Realist archetype:** Take a tender and gentle path through the paradox of change.

# ADVOCATE ARCHETYPE

The Advocate home is a special place that offers balance and stability to those who find their way to these spaces. The Advocate home is truly a trusted friend that reflects a message about being centered and being whole. It provides the right ground for someone to deal with core issues, emotional or otherwise. With an open heart, it fosters stillness and reflection.

The Advocate, by nature, feels a strong connection to those who live within its walls. It offers protection and support in a superbly gentle yet stable manner. Everyone feels at home with an Advocate archetype. Unlike other archetypes who may express themselves with some specific physical characteristics, this archetype is not defined by a certain style. It may be big or small, compact or sprawled—it could still have the Advocate energy.

Because the archetype is so committed to supporting the occupants, success is very possible here. Someone living with an Advocate may likely reach new heights in their career and become an expert in their field. This level of accomplishment is not due to business acumen but due to the level of support and encouragement that the Advocate offers. It is an unbridled champion for the goals and dreams of its occupants, no matter what they may want to accomplish.

The Advocate creates an environment where practical decisions are relatively easy to come by, yet does not support or expect hasty action. Rather its disposition is thoughtful, pragmatic, and evenly paced. Some may even consider the archetype a bit slow-moving. However, its primary concerns are the occupants and their corresponding achievements, without the pressure of a timeframe.

Of all the archetypes, the Advocate is the most selfless for they are positioned to offer whatever guidance they can. They make it easy for the occupants as well as visitors to find refuge with them. They love watching over whoever happens to be inside, sheltering from threatening weather as well as from threatening situations.

### Jeff and Jodie's supportive home

Jeff and Jodie were putting their home on the market, moving to a bigger one that would accommodate their growing family. They were both reluctant to leave but the necessity of having a larger space was apparent. There was no longer enough closet or storage space so they had spread out into their garage. With three children and another one on the way, they simply needed a bigger home in which to raise their family.

Jeff had bought the home when he was in his late 30s and still single. His hope of getting married and having children seemed like it might not happen at that point in his life, so he put his money into a home that he fell in love with at first sight. Reflecting back upon his life since moving in ten years prior, he realized how much had happened and how many of his dreams had come true.

Within a year of moving in, he met Jodie and was engaged. They had their small wedding in the backyard and the reception in the house. Their first baby arrived a year later. At his wife's encouragement, Jeff went back to school and finished his college degree, advancing his career and income substantially. A couple of years later, the twins arrived.

Meanwhile, Jodie, an English major, fulfilled a dream she had always nurtured which was to write a mystery novel. Eventually a publisher picked up the rights and she continues to draw royalties from the sale of her book. She is now writing a mystery series for which the publisher has already advanced her funds.

At the time of their move, Jeff and Jodie were expecting their fourth child. As they reminisced about how their lives had unfolded in the last ten years, they both agreed it had been a productive and creative time for them, both professionally and personally. Jodie had a special place in their home where she did her writing; Jeff had a place where he had not only studied for his degree but also currently did some work from home. The house had seen them through some enormous changes, providing them space and energy to do so. Their hope was that they could find another place with a similar feel which would support them in the same way so that their dreams would continue to be fulfilled.

Here is a case of a home holding the right space and energy for two people so that they could accomplish their goals in a steady and tenacious way. Typical of the Advocate home, they felt supported by it which, in turn, enabled them to support one another.

Although Jeff had no knowledge of the previous owners, he did know the house was built in 1960, which means it could be an Advocate home (1944–1963). Whether because of the previous owners, a remodel, or its natural affinity, the home expressed a balanced Advocate energy enabling them to take huge steps forward in their lives. How to speak to the Advocate: The best way to connect with your Advocate is through a quiet meditation or exercise. The physical symbols are not necessary, although they will be appreciated. A simple setting is preferred—a table with a candle or a single yellow flower is sufficient.

The Advocate will enjoy listening to your ideas and dreams

so be sure to share them all. You may not get advice as much as you'll get encouragement and continual support. As long as you live with the Advocate, you can be assured there will always be someone cheering you on.

**Challenges to occupants:** The downside for people living with an Advocate is the potential for getting caught up in their own problems and issues, thereby being unable to move forward with their plans. This archetype provides security and stability, but not wanting to sacrifice this safety net, occupants can become comfortable and thus avoid taking a new path, or making any changes. In order to avoid facing new challenges and experiences, they may move into self-doubt or apprehension.

**Feng Shui action to take:** Like the Protector archetype, the Advocate needs something to adjust if it has caused the occupants to get stuck. A working grandfather clock or a metal wind chime in the center of the space will symbolically reflect a continual and steady flow of movement. Although the wind-chime does not have to be rung, the grandfather clock must be working.

**Message of the Advocate archetype:** Empty your heart of the turmoil and find the still point.

> Buildings were to assist us in bringing the best of ourselves to the fore. They were to embalm our highest aspirations.
> —*The Architecture of Happiness,* Alain de Botton

# DIRECTOR ARCHETYPE

*Rosemary's inheritance*

Rosemary inherited her home from her parents. When they both died within a few months of one another, they made sure their home went to their only daughter. Rosemary moved in a few months after the second funeral. This was not the house she had grown up in and it wasn't a house she would have chosen, but it was paid for and it was hers.

Rosemary was a social worker and worked long hours. She also had two large dogs that were cared for by a dog walker during the week. Additionally, Rosemary's three sons, all in their 30s, made frequent visits back to see their mother, sometimes to stay overnight. There were times when they also brought friends, one was married, and one had a child that he often brought along. There was a lot of coming and going in Rosemary's life, which she loved.

Her parents' home, however, had been a quiet and orderly haven for them as they moved into their older years. Everything had its place and everything was immaculate. Rosemary saw the irony in moving into this place since she had never been the best housekeeper and never felt inclined to spend a lot of time hanging out at home. When she had free time, she went to a museum, a movie, or hung out with friends.

It didn't take long for her to realize that her lifestyle was not meshing with that of the house. She lived with chaos and with very little order. It had never been important to her to pick up or put things away and she doubted it ever would. When growing up, her parents had often discussed with her the messy state of her room, or the sloppy way she turned in her homework. Rosemary didn't care—it was all about living life to the fullest without the formalities.

She became less and less happy living in her parents' home and found lots of reasons to avoid going there. She hated to sell her house, not only out of respect for them, but also because it was paid for. Since it was kept in such impeccable condition, she couldn't foresee any upcoming expenses that she would have to undertake. There was no logical reason for her to move, other than that she was very unhappy.

Observing his mother's dilemma, her married son asked about buying the home from her. It had all the features they were looking for, plus they were getting ready to start their family. Would she consider selling the home to them? Rosemary knew the home would be in good hands because this son had not taken on her lackadaisical, carefree ways. She knew he and his wife would take care of it like her parents had done. She had never harmonized well with the home and could now find a different place better suited to her disposition.

The Director archetype is all about completion and culmination—of projects, ideas, business pursuits. This energy is disciplined and controlled and will foster the same in those who occupy its space. It has a natural tendency for intellectual pursuits and enjoys the stimulation of an academic environment as well as an efficient business organization. Someone living in a Director home may easily be a leader in the community or at their business.

It is not unusual for a different drummer to be keeping the beat in the Director home. Those who move into these homes should be prepared for this independent thinking to infiltrate their own lives. If they choose to step in time, new ventures await. Although independent, the Director is not haphazard in its approach. There's a methodical, logical, and precise attitude this archetype subscribes to which results in appropriate output.

Those who appreciate organization and competence will recognize what the Director can offer. This archetype expresses itself through the vehicle of order and structure. Its accomplishments are not necessarily tied to doing it in a certain way, but it must have some kind of framework in order to operate. Chaos and confusion are in direct opposition to the Director energy.

**How to speak to the Director:** The Director will respond well if you have planned an agenda for your connection with it. A short outline of what you want to accomplish and a tentative timeline will address this archetype's need for order. You may want to have a specific purpose for making contact; it will be difficult to connect if you have no real plan.

A crisp bell would summon the Director, but know that you will only need to ring it once or twice. If you'd rather have music in the background, a Bach fugue is suitable, playing to the Director's love of precision and mathematical interplays. Flowing, unstructured music will not be effective for this archetype.

Despite the seeming hard-edges to this archetype, once you have made the effort to contact and communicate, you will find a fascinating and reliable friend. Of all the archetypes, the Director is definitely the most cerebral but it will be genuinely curious about what interests you and how the two of you may find common ground. If you're living in a Director home, you probably already have plenty of common ground as this kind of collaboration isn't usually accidental.

**Challenges to occupants:** If a Director archetype veers off center, the admirable self-discipline qualities may become too rigid. Due to this lack of adaptability, a Director home can cause the occupants to become isolated, giving the impression of being aloof and distant. Although it can support and reflect a natural tendency to be a leader, this very leadership may lead to seclusion and separation if the Director archetype becomes unstable.

**Feng Shui action to take:** If rigid thought-patterns and overly disciplined behavior seem to be keeping someone from interacting well with coworkers, friends or family, the Director archetype may have gotten too exaggerated. To counteract, a picture of gently flowing water placed in the bedroom can help to soften the hard edges. A real fountain could also be effective if it doesn't disturb sleep.

**Message of the Director archetype:** Let your mind be still so you can remember the truth you have forgotten.

## INNOVATOR ARCHETYPE

The Innovator archetype carries over many of the knowledgeable and capable characteristics of the Director, but it also adds more creative and social aspects to its make-up. The Innovator home is often unique and clever with one-of-a-kind items and custom-designed pieces. The Innovator is not as formal or rigid as the Director, yet there is a definite sense of order, presented in a more light-hearted fashion. It reflects a lively and joyous vitality.

At times the Innovator seems to take on some extravagance in its appreciation of high quality surroundings. It is very discerning in its choices, not wanting to compromise excellence even if it costs more. Overall, however, the

Innovator exudes a comfortable, casual feel where visitors can be charmed by its distinctive flair. Because of this tendency towards individuality, the Innovator reflects independence and self-reliance to its occupants.

Visiting an Innovator home is a joyful and thoughtful experience as there will always be some touch of its unique playfulness to fascinate any visitors. This archetype will readily hold space for the residents to travel a path of self-exploration and inner development. This is a home that is great for artists, designers, and creative people in general. It will enable them to express their individual styles that are beneficial to both of them.

*Melanie's story*

After her divorce, Melanie moved into a new townhome with very little furniture, her clothes, and her cat. She agreed to let most of the furnishings remain with her ex-husband so she wouldn't be dragging reminders of a painful time into her new place. Once settled in, she began shopping for items to fill her home.

What she didn't expect is how fussy she suddenly became. Nothing was right—the fabric color was too light, too dark, the lines on the sofa were too straight, the headboard was the wrong shape. She hadn't ever observed herself being so fastidious. It seemed to take forever before she found the right side chair to go with her sofa, which in itself took months to find. But one by one she found what she was looking for and ended up with the right mix of some traditional looking pieces and some funky unique ones. Her space was beginning to make a statement.

Buying artwork was even more of a challenge for Melanie. In the past she would have bought some pre-framed posters and hung them wherever there was already a nail regardless of their size or their color. Not now. Melanie went to galleries, individual art shows, and she shopped on-line looking to find something unusual yet tasteful. It took her years in some cases to locate the right piece.

Her Innovator home reflected a strong statement about being a creative individual which did not go unnoticed by Melanie. She decided to take a class on glass blowing. Eventually she took more classes and became very proficient at the art, creating some interesting and conversational pieces that she displayed in her home. Melanie was asked to be part of an art exhibit at a local gallery which started a series of exhibits of her work. She has decided to pursue the art of glass blowing in a more professional way, creating an exit strategy from her current job as director of human resources.

**How to speak to the Innovator:** It is obvious the Innovator will appreciate a unique approach to establishing a relationship. It needs to be creative as well as thoughtful. What may work one time may not work the next so be prepared to approach the Innovator in different ways. It relishes a fresh tactic and will come to expect nothing less.

Drawing a picture of your home and framing it would be a personal and artistic way to connect. Creating a doll house that more or less replicates your Innovator home would be unique and unforgettable. Singing or playing a song written to your home would satisfy its need for individuality. As you can see, the Innovator is not happy with a token candle and some flowers. It is asking for something created by you.

If you're working on a project and need some original thoughts, the Innovator is adept at helping bring those forth. It doesn't settle for second-best yet will still infuse your endeavor with mischief and fun. It will not be boring living with an Innovator home.

**Challenges to the occupants:** The Innovator archetype could have a tendency to lead its occupants into being overly materialistic and overly confident. Although there is a natural propensity for this archetype to be sociable, the Innovator archetype can become obsessed with what people think of them as well as with being financially successful.

**Feng Shui action to take:** To bring the Innovator archetype back into its likeable and social nature and away from extremes, a large mirror hung near the front door will help the occupants recapture the joy and creativity inherent in their space. The mirror will enlarge the entrance, providing a bigger picture for those who live there.

**Message of the Innovator archetype:** Be mindful to keep your inner unity by consolidation rather than over-extension.

> The house has provided not only physical but also psychological sanctuary. It has been a guardian of identity. Over the years, its owners have returned from periods away and, on looking around them, remembered who they were.
> —*The Architecture of Happiness,* Alan de Botton

## MYSTIC ARCHETYPE

Mystic structures are infused with a sense of spirituality and strength. It reminds the occupants of the importance of contemplation and the development of inner resources. The Mystic has a quiet power that is reliable and stable so that those who are living with a Mystic will find themselves unconditionally supported. A Mystic home reminds its occupants of the importance of contemplation, enabling them to arrive at their own answers.

The Mystic is all about simplicity—which may be reflected in the floor plan and room arrangement. Typically it will be obvious by the use of simple lines in the furnishings and a lack of extraneous items. It also may reflect this concept of "less is more" in the lifestyle of its occupants who find themselves trying to make room for their own spiritual and emotional progress without getting caught up in outside diversions. This is an archetype that prefers a simple and wholesome way of life.

Mystic archetype homes are very connected to the earth and the planet. It is not unusual for occupants to become active in the green movement and attempt to incorporate as many of those principles as possible—from building materials to furnishings and cleaning supplies. True to the commitment of simplicity, incorporating ecological values is crucial to those living in a Mystic home.

Like a majestic mountain, the Mystic enables the occupants to ask "what next?" and then supports their climb to a higher level. Getting and maintaining the big picture is easier in the Mystic home because its own vision is vast and unimpeded by extraneous distractions.

*Nancy finds herself*

In the last year, Nancy had mourned the loss of her father and had gone through a sad and devastating divorce. She had married the man of her dreams, or so she thought, until he decided someone else was better suited to share his life. She moved out of their home to live with a friend until she could find a place of her own.

Nancy found a townhome to buy the first day she went out with her real estate agent. It was a very small two-bedroom place which didn't quite meet her spatial needs, but something about it was intriguing. Within two days of making an offer, the place was hers. The serious issue of moving into such a small space became reality.

Nancy purged and tossed, sorted and donated. In the end, she was able to move into the place with the belongings she had kept and found appropriate and adequate spots for everything. The place seemed made for her scaled-down life. Some items Nancy moved expecting she'd had to get rid of them once she was there, but they found a place to land. She was nicely surprised at the adaptability of the little townhome.

Nancy found instant refuge in her new place. She never felt cramped or crowded but rather discovered that living in this small place was refreshing and simple. She could concentrate on her own healing and ponder her next step. She didn't have to figure out furniture arrangements since the furniture could only go one way. She didn't have to worry about all the time it would take to scrub out rows of cupboards or rooms of closets—in one day she had managed to get them up to her standards.

This was a place in which Nancy could journal and pray, meditate and process her two major losses. She had time to take a yoga class and to be by herself. She discovered how much she loved her home and how easy it was for her to be alone. She refrained from entertaining much, not because of the size of her place, but because she simply enjoyed the quiet and the sacredness she found in those walls. She was finding her way back to wholeness.

Several years later Nancy met another man. They dated for a while before she felt comfortable enough to invite David to her home. The first time he walked in, he knew immediately why she had kept him away. He could tell this place meant everything to her. It was as though she had opened her soul to him. He had the insight to know how reverent this place was to Nancy and shared with her that he felt as though he was walking on sacred ground.

Nancy moved out of her townhome when she and David got married. There was no way two people could live in the small space. Although she was happy to move on with her life and actually have some storage space for a change, she often thinks back with fondness on her years in that tiny home. She still considers it a mystical place that helped her through some difficult times.

**How to speak to the Mystic:** The Mystic would appreciate and support a space clearing ceremony to set the stage for a strong and meaningful connection. This clearing can be done throughout the whole home or just in a specific area. Using incense or a bell along with your focused intention, a space can be cleared of any energetic disturbances. Like tuning in a radio to get clearer reception, a space clearing tunes in a space.

The Mystic will probably not advise you on the smaller details of your life but will instead offer some insightful and meaningful thoughts about the big picture. Rather than expecting an answer about how to deal with an issue, you can expect a more cosmic approach that asks why you're dealing with the issue in the first place.

**Challenges to the occupants:** Those living in a Mystic archetype home can find themselves on an endless search for answers. Whether seeking advice from gurus, following a new line of thinking, or looking for alternatives to health issues, the Mystic archetype home may support this everlasting hunt for options and solutions.

**Feng Shui action to take:** In order to bring focus into those who are under the influence of the over-charged Mystic archetype, bring a dark color into the bedroom. A dark green, purple, or navy, will corral the tendency to embark on an outer quest and support a more inner search.

**Message of the Mystic Archetype:** Give yourself to the present moment and still the mind.

# Additional Stories

Presented below are two stories exemplifying the dynamic experience of archetypes playing out in the home. In the first example, the established archetype of the home changes to fit the preferences of the couple. This did not occur until after a long and arduous remodel project. The second example shows how different house archetypes played out while the occupant tried to culminate her dream.

### Changing the archetype of the home
*Lyle and Louise's story*

Lyle and Louise bought a home after Lyle was eligible for an early retirement. Their reasoning was that they would have a "project" since the house needed a lot of restoration and since they were not ready to slow down their pace. They also wanted to provide enough room for their three children and five grandchildren, if and when they all would come to visit.

They moved from a home they had designed and built themselves right after they got married. It was everything they had wanted in a home. There was adequate storage so there was a place for everything. The room arrangement was efficient and accommodated their lifestyle. The feature they loved the best was their library, where they could store all their books from floor to ceiling. Both Lyle and Louse instilled in their children the importance of study and education. The library was their pride and joy and a great place for the children to study.

They appreciated fine art and had collected a few valuable items. They both also believed in the importance of music, so their home was filled with both modern as well as antique instruments. They enjoyed private music evenings when all five of them were together and would become an impromptu "band." After the children left home, Lyle and Louise stayed in their home for a few years. It was after Lyle retired from his job that it became obvious they needed more to their lives, so they looked to find another outlet for themselves. They bought a larger home that they felt would give them a chance to be creative and accommodate their expanding family.

The previous owners to their new purchase were a couple who had lived in the house for over seventy years before both of them died of old age. The husband had been raised in the house and acquired it after his parents died. Lyle and Louise bought it from their grown children. The children had kept the house for several years after the death of their parents, unsure

about what to do with it. They all had fond memories of growing up there and weren't eager to let it go. The children rented
it out for a while, however the renters eventually defaulted on
the rent, not before causing a lot of destruction to the place.
The house remained empty for another couple of years.

Lyle and Louise felt drawn to take it on but from the very
start things did not go well. The first night they stayed in the
house, Louise had a meltdown about the amount of work they
had gotten themselves into, how long it would all take, and
how much money it would cost. They discussed the ramifications of what they had done until the early morning hours.
Lyle was unable to make a convincing argument since he, too,
was struck with the enormity of the project.

Nevertheless, they persevered. They began working on the
house, doing as much of the work as they could by themselves.
Over the years, their marriage faltered; they argued over costs,
design decisions, and how much to hire out. One of their sons
moved back home for a couple years, causing further irrita-
tion and arguments. A niece of Louise's was attending a college
close by and asked about living in their home, despite the
remodeling, while she finished the last two years of school. It
seemed like a plumber, contractor or electrician was always in
their home doing the parts they chose not to do themselves.
For two people who had hoped to quietly live in a beautiful historical home, restoring it little-by-little to its original
beauty, moving into this place turned into a ten-year night-
mare, with little privacy, small amounts of satisfaction, and
definitely no relaxation.

Suddenly one morning, Lyle and Louise were having
breakfast and doing what they had done for ten years—sorting

through their house file to see what project they needed to bulldoze through next. That morning they realized their home restoration project was done. Of course, a few details here and there remained to be completed, but all the big projects were over. Having been in the midst of the battle for so long, neither one had looked up long enough to measure their progress.

Marking this momentous realization, they walked through their home together, reminiscing about the various projects, taking pride in how their hard work had paid off, and admiring the beauty of their home. It was as though a page turned and they began to read a different story—one which they were familiar with and one which they enjoyed. They were reading a story that reflected them.

Several explanations could be given for why Lyle and Louise struggled so much in their new home and then why the circumstances suddenly improved. A Feng Shui analysis would say that the predecessor energy negatively impacted their experience. Having renters isn't always a ticket to disaster, but often it simply is. Some renters do not have the commitment to a place that owners do, and so therefore don't take care of it with the same concern. Also the next generation of owners themselves was reluctant to sell because of their fond memories. They continued to have a connection to the space and would keep it even if it was abused—the house was still a part of their lives. Either of those two issues would be sufficient to have set up roadblocks to Lyle and Louise's intention to make it their home. Predecessor energy alone can determine whether someone will enjoy their home or hate living there.

Lyle and Louise were also struggling with the archetype of this new home that was so vastly different from what they were accustomed to living with. From their lifestyle, it appears their former home had a formidable amount of Director characteristics—structure, organization, educational focus. The Director, by its very nature, fosters self-discipline and self-control, along with a sense of order. But even more importantly, it supports a private and more inward direction.

The fixer-upper home that they bought fits the Protector profile which is to protect and gather people. This, of course, was not the intention of our ambitious couple, who only wanted a project they could work on together—just the two of them. Over the course of time, they not only had workmen and contractors in their space on a continual basis, but also other relatives. Furthermore, the Protector home is much more adept at dealing with chaos and loose ends, concentrating more on the welfare of the people rather than the physical environment. This, of course, was not how Lyle and Louise had been accustomed to living their lives. Although it all worked out, the anxiety brought on by moving from a Director home to that of a Protector took some adjustments they hadn't expected.

So how did they come to terms with this Protector archetype since it didn't suit them? Why did they even agree to buy the home in the first place when it was clearly so different than their current one? The second question addresses a common situation where people buy a home and then regret that they did. It's as though an unseen force is propelling them into circumstances that will provide valuable lessons and a chance to expand awareness. These lessons in awareness are probably not going to be fun and, if left up to our practical minds, are something we would naturally avoid. If logic was the only factor, Lyle and Louise would have seen the work involved and the possible problems they could encounter and would have backed away. However, buying a home is a very emotional decision—they leapt to the part where their growing family would all be together and skipped the part about how that would happen.

The first question about how they came to terms with the Protector archetype addresses another common phenomenon. It was obvious Lyle and Louise flourished with the Director archetype which was expressed in their original home. It allowed them to convey themselves fully in a way that was comfortable and appropriate to their preferences. They assumed this same energy would simply follow them to the next place. But it didn't. Another archetype was playing out in the new home and that is when the problems began.

What happened with Lyle and Louise is that eventually their new home relinquished the Protector tendencies and took on those of a Director. One way an archetype can change is when there has been extensive remodeling—when the physical structure has changed and improved so much that it is hard to recognize its original intent. Lyle and Louise did accomplish this. A partial list of their remodeling projects included: modernizing the kitchen; turning a bedroom into a master bathroom; enclosing a back porch; restoring the wood floors, woodwork and banister; replacing windows; adding an energy efficient furnace. Such a drastic transformation set the platform for a drastic energy change as well; the home changed archetypes. It changed to an archetype that was more fitting for the current owners—which is what made them feel as though they were finally "at home."

## Living with different archetypes

*Joan's story*

It took *Joan* eight years and three homes before she completed her doctoral degree. In hindsight she realized the idea came to her while she was living in a Visionary archetype home. She was a successful marriage counselor when she bought her home. It wasn't long after moving in that the idea of getting her doctorate became a driving force.

Joan was excited to start the journey knowing it would take time and effort before she attained her degree since she needed to continue working. The first few years she found her coursework fascinating and stimulating and it was intellectually challenged. But for some unknown reason, she lost focus and took a leave from her studies.

At the same time she married her long-time beau and they moved into a home they bought together. It was in this house that Joan found the energy and support to return to her studies. She picked up where she had left off. She didn't have the enthusiastic excitement that she had at the beginning of her program, but she moved forward with an ample degree of commitment and support. With great satisfaction, Joan slowly and steadily progressed with her thesis until it was close to being completed.

However, she was not to get the coveted degree in this house. It wasn't because she gave up on it due to lack of interest. Rather, she seemed to be working on it endlessly, reworking her perspective, rewording her arguments. She seemed caught on a never-ending wheel that wouldn't let her get off. It wasn't until Joan and her husband moved again to another home that she easily brought an end to her studies. As though blinders had been removed, Joan discovered where she had been stuck, got her thesis approved and, within a year and a half, had her degree.

Discussions with Joan about her sequential homes and their influence on her final accomplishment led to a revealing observation of the impact of the archetypes. Joan began the journey toward her doctorate while under the influence of the Visionary archetype. Characteristic of the Visionary energy, she was inspired to get going and move forward with her plans. However, the space got her going but wasn't able to sustain the endeavor, evidenced by Joan losing interest. The Visionary archetype can move into overwhelm and lack of focus.

The next home moved her forward yet, at the same time, kept her stuck. This is typical of an Advocate home that would help and support Joan in her dream of getting her doctorate. But, in this case, the Advocate was also out of balance and was not able to support her until the end of her project. It wasn't until Joan and her husband moved into a Director home, with its innate sense of discipline and its need to bring closure and completion, which enabled her to quickly and easily complete her degree.

If Joan had been aware of how to work with archetypes of homes, she could have implemented a Feng Shui adjustment in the first house (Visionary) that may have brought about the culmination of her doctorate while she was still living there. If not in that home, she could have placed a Feng Shui adjustment for her second home (Advocate) that may have kept her from successfully getting her degree. As it turned out, her third home brought her the desired goal.

## Last thoughts about archetypes
To further enhance your work with archetypes, think back to a childhood home to see if you can determine whether its

archetype is similar or vastly different from the home you're currently occupying. Perhaps you were better suited to your home growing up, or it may be you're living with an archetype that is identical to the one of your childhood. Making comparisons between the past and the present archetypes can be helpful to you, clarifying your reasons for feeling comfortable or for feeling right at home in your current place.

You can also determine the archetype of a home you lived in during a past marriage and compare it to where you are now. If you're still living in the same home after your divorce, you may want to explore whether the archetype of the house changed during the trauma of the split between you and your spouse. As your children leave, take note as to whether the archetype changes there as well. When a family member comes to live with you, such as a parent, does the archetype of your home change?

# Putting It All Together

The intention of *Conversations with Your Home* is to provide you ways to connect and communicate with your home in order to deepen your understanding of its unique energy. So that you're not overwhelmed about where to start, here is a suggested fast-track plan of action, highlighting the basic steps to take to start making a connection to your home:

A preliminary exercise is to start a scrapbook for your home. It can be the holding place for the exercises you do to connect with your space as well as a place to put practical items, like blueprints, deed, photographs, letters, etc. It will be a reference for you as you put together the story of your home: Scrapbook for your home (page 13).

The first section is **Psychology of Space.** Here you will discover how psychologically your space influences you and how it rounds out who you are. This section underlines the idea that your space is actively engaging with you, whether you're aware of its influence or not. You can determine its involvement in your next step forward by the following exercise: Is my house leading me to my future? (page 23).

In the second section called **Stages of Sanctuary,** you will find ways to establish your relationship with your home. There are various exercises you can do, some are situation-specific, for example, if you're just building or you are about to move. You may find some of the exercises do not apply now but may be appropriate later. The goal is to use the exercises that are relevant in order to establish communication with your home. Suggested exercises are:

Naming your home (page 80)
Writing a letter to your home (page 88)
Photographing your home (page 108)

**Symbols of Soul** is the third section that introduces the groundbreaking idea that your home can be identified with an archetype. What this implies is that your home has had prior influences which, in turn, influence you. Here is where to start with regard to determining your home's archetype:

Discovering the archetype of your home questionnaire (page 138)

By determining the archetype(s) of your home, you have prepared yourself to have a deeper and clearer channel of communication. Take the quiz to see which archetype appears.

All three sections of *Conversations with Your Home* are intended to guide you in opening your eyes to a simple yet profound idea that your home is truly alive. As you deepen your awareness, your home becomes a friend that guides and supports you. The bottom line is that we live in our homes and they, in turn, live in us.

Because this is a reciprocal relationship, as you succeed, so does your home. By following your heart's song, you will influence your home in a positive, heartfelt way, helping it to realize its own dreams.

> John Ruskin (1819–1900, art critic, poet, artist, social thinker) proposed that we seek two things of our buildings. We want them to shelter us. And we want them to speak to us—to speak of whatever we find important and need to be reminded of.
> —*The Architecture of Happiness,* Alan de Botton

# Addendum A

## Explanation for Age of House Numbers

Chinese astrology plays an integral role in the implementation of traditional Feng Shui. Not only is a proper location or space important for good Feng Shui, but a proper time should be in place as well. One aspect of time consideration includes the Heavenly Stems, otherwise known as the 5 Elements: Fire, Earth, Metal, Water, and Wood. The Chinese felt that the interaction of the Elements was responsible for everything in the universe. The progression of these Elements can represent seasons, directions, days and hours, or any event for that matter. They are symbolic representations of the cycle of natural phenomena, depicting the flow of a phase from beginning to culmination, stepping through each of the Elements.

Along with this heavenly aspect of time, there is also an earthly factor known as the 12 Earthly Branches, or the 12 animals of the Chinese zodiac (rat, ox, tiger, etc.). These, too, represent a cycle of time. Each two-hour increment of a day has a corresponding animal sign, as does each month and each year.

When the five Heavenly Stems and the twelve Earthly Branches are combined, there are 60 possible combinations. The most common application of this coupling system is used for the description of years. It takes 60 years to complete a full cycle before there's a duplication of a Stem and Branch pairing.

In addition, the Taoists viewed the universe as having three components: heaven, earth, and humanity, also known as the 3 Treasures. The three-component model permeated all parts of the Taoist life, so it would follow that rather than considering each 60-year cycle in isolation, there would be three of these, for a total of 180 years (called Upper, Middle, Lower Periods). In the same vein, the 60 years could be divided into thirds, comprised of 20-year segments (simply called a Period).

Since the number 3 holds importance, three times 3 would be even more consequential. The number 9 not only implies three 3s but also is the highest single-digit number before returning to 0 or 1, so it represents completeness and perfection. The Forbidden City originally had 9,999 rooms. Each of its main entry doors has 81 gold knobs attached to the surface. Nine mythical animals sit on the eaves of the imperial buildings. Therefore, each of the 20-year phases was assigned a number from 1 to 9.

Switching from ancient Chinese calendars to Western calendars accounts for why the periods are not divided by decades. When exactly the practice of numbering the years began has not been determined, however, at the time of this writing we are in a No. 8 period (2010). There will be one more period after this (2024–2043, Period 9), after which the numbers will begin again with No. 1.

AGE OF HOUSE AND CORRESPONDING PERIOD DESIGNATION
Northern Hemisphere
     1844–1863 – Period 9
     1864–1883 – Period 1
     1884–1903 – Period 2
     1904–1923 – Period 3
     1924–1943 – Period 4
     1944–1963 – Period 5

1964–1983 – Period 6
1984–2003 – Period 7
2004–2023 – Period 8

# The Five Elements

Each of the 20-year Periods also has a connection to a Chinese concept called the 5 Elements. The Element system originated as the delineation of the conditions needed to support their agrarian society. The Elements are: Water, Wood, Earth, Fire, and Metal. Wood represents the crops or plants. Water is needed to assure the growth of the plants. Earth is needed to nurture and support the growth of the plans. The ash from Fire is used to enrich the soil; Metal tools are required to hoe, trim, and rake the plants. A successful crop required the use of all 5 Elements.

Over time, the Element system evolved and expanded in its usage. It integrated into hierarchical relationships between each of the Elements. One expression of this hierarchy is the supportive cycle: Water helps Wood to grow; Wood stokes up the Fire; Fire enriches the Earth; Earth produces Metals; and Metal produces Water in the form of condensation. The other relationship cycle is a controlling one: Water controls Fire; Fire melts Metal; Metal chops down Wood: Wood depletes Earth; and Earth dams up Water. When a particular Element is depleted or overcharged, another Element can either support it or control it, depending on the specific case.

Eventually the Elements became associated with the directions, seasons, hours of the day, months of the year and the zodiac animals. The system is a crucial underpinning of Feng Shui with different areas of the space or property representing a particular Element. In today's modern society, the Elements have been a method for identifying personality attributes; they have been utilitzed for building an organizational team, and even for selecting clothes.

Each of the Elements is an archetype in its own right which identifies and labels a universal force.

**Water:** Without a shape of its own, water is the poster-child for flexibility. Water adapts, yields, and accommodates, exemplifying a common water phrase about "going with the flow." It is the most introspective of the Elements yet, like a still lake, has a depth and strength that challenges its yielding qualities. Just as water will eventually erode a mountain, the Water element can bring about fierce changes in a quiet and invisible way.

When Water loses its balance in the cycle, it can become undefined and unable to hold its strength. It becomes "wishy-washy" and requires Wood to take away some of the excess Water. One suggestion to offset the effects of it being overly active in an environment would be to add a plant.

**Wood:** Wood supports action. It clarifies the vision and moves things forward. There's a decisive and almost impetuous quality to the energy of Wood, yet it has the ability to flex and bend (as in bamboo) when met with resistance. Like the small bud that struggles through the snow reaching for sunlight, Wood energy is purposeful and often driven; it loves to be challenged; it pushes the limits and is on a persistent quest to be first.

Too much Wood results in the initiation of too many ideas, projects, or experiences preventing appropriate completion of things initiated. Just as planting too many tulip bulbs in a small area doesn't allow any of them the adequate space to blossom, too much Wood in a situation chokes out any chances of expansion and growth. The Element that can bring Wood back into balance is Metal (a metal windchime or a round shape).

**Fire:** Fire provides energy and excitement. It is passionate and dynamic. Like Wood, it is expansive but in more directions and with more exuberance. Fire is catalytic, bringing about change as though by magic. It can change cold to heat, it can melt hard materials into pliable ones, it can blend various aspects of a recipe to make a delicious mixture. As a fire warms the chilly night, it emits a mesmerizing hypnotic effect. Everyone is drawn to the magic of a fire.

When Fire gets too much energy behind it, it can become overly exuberant and intense. There's a need to move away to prevent getting burned or scorched. While a fire in a fireplace can heat a home, left uncontained it can burn the house down. The Element that can keep Fire from losing control is Earth. Therefore, installing brick or marble in a key area will add the Earth element.

**Earth:** The Earth element brings nurturing and comfort, peace and stabilization. Like Fire, it is very magnetic but for a different reason—it is nonthreatening and gentle. Earth energy is grounding, centering, and receptive. Of all of the Elements, it is Earth that receives and gladly accepts the seedlings and bulbs to support their growth. The Planet Earth and Earth Mother are all titles for an energy that is embracing and accepting.

When Earth is no longer in balance its energy can feel heavy and weighted down. The extra baggage associated with this excess might be expressed as feeling "buried" or "in a rut." The

Metal element or the Water element is a good balance for too much Earth. The Metal requirement can be a metal windchime or an object that is round; the Water element can be a mirror.

**Metal:** The Metal element brings decisive action and measured quality. It cuts through the superfluous and streamlines; it clears away the clutter and simplifies. Just as a metal tool would prune a tree or rake up the dead leaves, Metal is adept at bringing closure when needed and discarding the redundant or excessive. As its name suggests, Metal energy can be reminiscent of clanking coins or jingling jewels—a powerful metaphor for its inherent relation to abundance.

When Metal becomes unbalanced and excessive, there can be a tendency for rigidity and perfectionism. The overly-zealous Metal may "cut off" any other possibilities or suggestions, coming from the belief that there's only one way to take action or resolve an issue. The Water element is a good balancing agent when Metal gets too "edgy" or cold. A picture of water or a fountain is a good suggestion for Metal that has run amok.

The Elements for each of the 20-Year Periods are:

> 1844–1863 – Magician (fire)
> 1864–1883 – Adaptor (water)
> 1884–1903 – Protector (earth)
> 1904–1923 – Visionary (wood)
> 1924–1943 – Realist (wood)
> 1944–1963 – Advocate (earth)
> 1964–1983 – Director (metal)
> 1984–2003 – Innovator (metal)
> 2004–2023 – Mystic (earth)

If your home was built prior to 1844, the cycle repeats itself so that 1824–1843 homes are Mystic (earth); 1804–1823 homes are Innovator (metal), etc.


# Addendum B

# What is Feng Shui?

Although the focus of *Conversations with Your House* is not Feng Shui, the premise of the book came about because of this ancient Asian system of thought. For those who are interested in further information about the concept, I offer a basic introduction below. For even more on the topic, please refer to my prior two books as listed on the References.

Feng Shui identifies and influences the circulation and flow of the life force (ch'i) in an environment. The goal in implementing Feng Shui is to create balance and harmony in a working or living space. This ancient Chinese concept provides ways to create or select an ideal space that will bring the occupant prosperity, productivity, and overall good luck.

Feng Shui gives a new perspective for viewing life by considering the influence of the surrounding environment. It supports change. It can change lives. In many cases Feng Shui involves just plain common sense: if the faucet is leaking, call a plumber; if a light bulb is burned out, replace it; if a door sticks, fix it. However, the Chinese have a poetic way of looking at literal issues. In addition to the mundane changes, using the Feng Shui principle that your space mirrors your life, you may ask what besides the faucet is "leaking" out of your life; where else are you "burned out," what issue is "sticky" for you right now. Along that same line of thought, if you want to call someone or something into your life, use a bell or chime by your entry. If you want to stop money from running out the front door, put an empty basket inside the door to catch the flow of wealth before it leaves your house. If you want some project or relationship to blossom, place a healthy lush plant on your nightstand to represent growth and vitality.

The adjustments for Feng Shui can be small and subtle and are usually affordable. An adjustment may not even be visible—a mirror placed in a closet or a business card tucked behind a picture can be as effective as rearranging the living room furniture. The power of the adjustment does not depend on the object as much as the intention with which the object was placed. Being unclear about what you're trying to accomplish with the windchime or the plant will not maximize the results you hope to achieve using Feng Shui. Your environment needs to speak of your clear and focused intention in order for you to make the changes you want in your life.

Feng Shui is a process. As with your own growth emotionally, mentally, and spiritually, you will never be done. This is not meant to be discouraging but to make you aware that, as your life continues to change, so will your environment. Since your space reflects your life, it too will undergo some changes. Anytime anything in your surroundings changes, so do you. Acknowledging the direct link between the inner world and the outer world is the power that Feng Shui provides. If you cannot find peace in your home because there's nowhere you can go to be quiet, or because there's unfinished business all over, clutter stacked up in piles, and invasive noises, then you won't be able to deal very well with the battles going on inside. On inner levels you will also be dealing with unfinished business, clutter in the form of too many activities and too many people making demands, and noise from the chatter going on in your mind. The support from your space, as it reflects back to you what changes you've made on the inside, helps you confront and face what is waiting for you in the outer world.

There are two main schools of Feng Shui, both of which are effective and valid. From a more traditional perspective, the positive and negative factors of a site are determined by the use a compass which then analyzes the directional influence on the occupants in relation to their space. Each of the eight areas represents one of the directions. Along with the center, they are carefully scrutinized for potential issues. A more modern approach, called Black Sect Tantric Buddhist Feng Shui, uses a mental map called a bagua, which replaces the compass.

It, too, determines the eight areas plus the center, however, the location of the specific areas is established by the position of the front door, not by an alignment with the direction.

Both Feng Shui schools relate these nine areas to a life issue, using the same terminology: Career (north), Knowledge (northeast), Family (east), Wealth (southeast), Fame and Reputation (south), Relationships (southwest), Children and Creativity (west), and Helpful People (northwest), with Health being in the center of a space. Once the occupant determines a specific issue or issues, the physical location that represents that issue is found in the space, and a corresponding physical change is made in that area.

A change can mean adding a new object, like a plant or a fountain. It may involve something bigger, like putting up a wall or changing a door. Making a change in the space could also mean fixing something—a window that doesn't open, a door that squeaks, a faucet that drips, a cupboard door that doesn't open easily. Making a change could also mean removing something, especially if the object has a negative meaning for the occupant. An old boyfriend gives you a sweater that, although beautiful and expensive, reminds you of a painful time in your life. Just because something has positive aesthetic qualities doesn't mean it will benefit someone. A change can mean getting rid of pervasive clutter as well, which could be holding someone back.

You cannot control the world, but Feng Shui enables you to control your personal space. It is a powerful way to bring balance and harmony to your life. Based on the premise that your space is a mirror for what is going on in your life, Feng Shui can help you see your space as well as your life with new eyes.

By changing your space, a corresponding change will occur in some aspect of your life—career, money, health, relationship, etc. When your space impacts you positively, you can move forward with confidence and an assurance of success.

# References

Bachelard, Gaston. *The Poetics of Space: The Classic Look at How We Experience Intimate Places.* Beacon Press (Boston). 1958.

Barrie, Thomas. *Spiritual Path, Sacred Place: Myth, Ritual, and Meaning in Architecture.* Shambhala (Boston & London). 1996.

Cooper Marcus, Clare. *House as a Mirror of Self: Exploring the Deeper Meaning of Home.* Conari Press (Berkeley, CA). 1995.

deBotton, Alan. *The Architecture of Happinesss.* Vintage International (NY). 2006.

Emoto, Masaru. *The Message from Water.* IHM (Japan). 1999.

Hyder, Carole. *Wind & Water: Your Personal Feng Shui Journey.* Hyder Enterprises, Inc. (Minneapolis). 1998.

Hyder, Carole. *Living Feng Shui: Personal Stories.* Hyder Enterprises, Inc. (Minnesota). 2001.

Jung, Carl G. *Memories, Dreams, and Reflections.* Vintage Books (New York). 1961.

Lawlor, Anthony. *The Temple in the House.* G.P. Putnam's Sons (New York). 1994.

Lulic, Margaret. *Home—Inspired by Love and Beauty.* Blue Edge Publishing (Minneapolis). 2010.

# Acknowledgments

My life would certainly have taken a different turn if I had not gone to Berkeley, California, back in 1992 and met a man who changed everything. His Holiness Grandmaster Lin Yun introduced me to what would become my life's journey down a Feng Shui path and I have never looked back. I am grateful for the evolutionary work he and Her Holiness Rinpoche Crystal Chu have done to blend the traditional Feng Shui perspective with the modern world, making it accessible to all.

A special thank you goes to my writing buddy, Margaret Lulic. We logged many hours together and bounced many ideas around before our respective books emerged. I am grateful for her patience and her guidance during some less-than-pretty moments. It has been a pleasure and an inspiration to work with someone who holds clarity and integrity as their focus. Thank you, dear friend.

Thank you to my readers and contributors. Janet Sawyer slogged her way through the initial manuscript, offering advice in subtle and not-so-subtle ways. I appreciate the time that it l took and am grateful for her conscientious attention to what I was trying to accomplish. Thanks to Lisa Janusz who used her editorial eye and professional expertise to help me confirm and clarify some of the text. I appreciate the thoughtful contribution of personal stories by Theresa and Dorine.

To Carie Gross, who designed the cover—always a joy to work with her. I love the way her mind thinks. Someday we'll have to meet!

Once again, I had the joy of working with Dorie McClelland, book designer and cheerleader. I think I write books just so I can work with her! Her editing, insights, and design ideas are superb. She is a blessing in my life.

I don't know how I will ever be able to thank my husband Tom. He has read the entire book and parts of it countless times in the many different versions it went through before settling into final form. His gentle suggestions, insightful ideas, and undying support gave me the nudge I needed at just the right moment. Thank you, sweetheart, for being here through the darkness and the sunlight.

Finally, thank you to my house which clearly inspired me to connect in ways I wouldn't have done on my own. It is an honor to live within its walls and be inspired by its own story. I hope that you, dear reader, will likewise be inspired in your own way to connect with your space and make the exhilarating discovery for yourself that, indeed, your house is waiting to have a conversation with you.

# Carole J. Hyder
International Feng Shui Expert

## Available for
## Workshops, Speaking Engagements,
## and Training

Carole is founder of the
# Wind & Water School of Feng Shui
Since 1998 the School has been
certifying individuals to take
Feng Shui into homes and offices.

**For more information about Carole,
go to www.carolehyder.com**

**For more information about the School,
go to www.windwaterschool.com**

# Don't Stop Now!

If you appreciated this book consider the following:

Read *Home—Inspired by Love and Beauty* by Margaret A. Lulic, M.A. This holistic book explores how a house becomes a home that enriches its people with beauty, peace, happiness, self-discovery, health and well-being through simple actions and your own inspiration.

Whether you are new to creating your own living space and lasting relationships or have done so for decades, you will find refreshing insights and practical suggestions in this thought-provoking book. She demonstrates how a loving relationship with your home rewards singles, couples, and their children. And you'll be absolutely touched by her heartfelt message.

Margaret Lulic and I have been writing partners for these two wonderful books drawing on each other for wisdom, inspiration, and support so that they may serve you with the best information and insights from a diverse world of experience.

Margaret's book is available at LulicBooks.com.

*Margaret Lulic and Carole Hyder*

*Excerpt from:*

## Home—Conceived in Love and Beauty

### Welcome Home

A loving home is the unity of a specific dwelling, all those people and things that it shelters, and the sense of treasuring and being treasured. In its fullest form, everything about the home has been conceived in love and inspired by beauty—not just the physical aspects—but the relationships, values, and daily rituals. The result is the happiness that Aristotle argues is the deepest desire of humanity. This is not just the happiness of pleasure or peace of mind; it is the happiness of participation in something meaningful. The act of conceiving arises from your inner life of imagination, understanding, and creativity. It pervades every aspect of your special place and your interaction with it, starting with your return.

When do you feel you have returned home? Is it as you see your familiar site from the street corner or pull into your driveway? Is it as you open the back door, fold your arms around a loved one, or sink into your favorite chair? Perhaps the answer changes with circumstances. I have different moments that ring the bell of my heart and announce, "I'm home."

. . . Our homes have tremendous potential to nurture and heal us, to help us grow, and to surround us with beauty and harmony as well as those we love. Today, homes are a great treasure for far more people than ever before in history, but the meaning of home has changed considerably over the centuries. By the later part of the 20th century the new field of environmental psychology, the science of place, asserts that your behavior and the places within which it occurs are an integrated unit. Describing one without the other is capturing only part of the picture. Winifred Gallagher, author of The Power of Place and House Thinking, would explain that "not unlike medicines, places have effects, and that when accurately 'prescribed,' they can make us feel better."

Clare Cooper Marcus, in her book *House as a Mirror of Self* points out that part of our human development involves meaningful relationships with significant physical environments as well as with people. Home has not received enough attention because all the typical fields of study slice and dice the world in ways that do not take into account what is one of our greatest emotional connections. Welcome to a journey into this world where we will draw on insights from many fields but most importantly from people who love their homes.